## RESEARCH CENTER BOOKS OF RELATED INTEREST

ENTRANCE TO THE ZOHAR, compiled and edited by Dr. Philip S. Berg

ENTRANCE TO THE TREE OF LIFE, compiled and edited by Dr. Philip S. Berg

REINCARNATION: THE WHEELS OF A SOUL, by Dr. Philip S. Berg (also edited in Hebrew, Spanish, French, Russian and Persian)

KABBALAH FOR THE LAYMAN I, by Dr. Philip S. Berg (also edited in Hebrew, Spanish, French, Russian, German, Persian, Chinese and Portuguese)

KABBALAH FOR THE LAYMAN II, by Dr. Philip S. Berg (also edited in Hebrew and French)

KABBALAH FOR THE LAYMAN III, by Dr. Philip S. Berg

TEN LUMINOUS EMANATIONS, vol. 1, compiled and edited by R. Levi Krakovsky (also edited in Hebrew)

TEN LUMINOUS EMANATIONS, vol. 2, compiled and edited by Dr. Philip S. Berg (also edited in Hebrew)

LIGHT OF REDEMPTION, by R. Levi Krakovsky

GENERAL PRINCIPLES OF KABBALAH, by R. M. Luzatto

GIFT OF THE BIBLE, by R. Yehudah Ashlag (also edited in Hebrew)

THE KABBALAH CONNECTION, by Dr. Philip S. Berg (also edited in Spanish)

ASTROLOGY: THE STAR CONNECTION, by Dr. Philip S. Berg (also edited in Hebrew, French and Spanish)

ZOHAR: PARASHAT PINHAS, vols.1, 2 and 3 translated and edited by Dr. Philip Berg

POWER OF THE ALEPH BETH, vols. 1 and 2 by Dr. Philip S. Berg

## BOOKS IN PRINT

AQUARIAN EXPRESS: THE NEW AGE AND YOU, by Dr. Philip S. Berg

KABBALISTIC MEDITATION, by Dr. Philip S. Berg

TEN LUMINOUS EMANATIONS, vol. 3 compiled and edited by Dr. Philip S. Berg

ASK YOUR BOOKSELLER FOR THE BOOKS AND TAPES YOU HAVE MISSED

# Time Zones

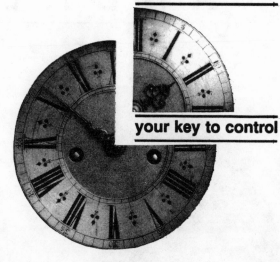

**your key to control**

# KABBALAH

**Research Centre of Kabbalah**

J e r u s a l e m — N e w  Y o r k

# *Time Zones*

## your key to control

# Dr. Philip S. Berg

FIRST EDITION
February 1990


ISBN 0-924457-00-7 (Hardcover)
ISBN 0-924457-01-5 (Softcover)


*For further information, address:*


RESEARCH CENTRE OF KABBALAH
200 PARK AVENUE, SUITE 303E
NEW YORK, N.Y. 10017


— or —


RESEARCH CENTRE OF KABBALAH
P.O.BOX 14168
THE OLD CITY, JERUSALEM


PRINTED IN U.S.A.

1990

*This book is dedicated*

## *to my wife Lea*

*who has been the inspiration*

*to bring me to the Light*

*and to my children*

## *Daniel and Jonathan*

*who support me*

*For My Wife*

## Karen

*In the vastness of cosmic space*

*and*

*the infinity of lifetimes,*

*it is my bliss to share*

*a soulmate and an age of Aquarius with you*

# ACKNOWLEDGEMENT

*I would like to express my gratitude to Robert L. Fischer for compiling, reviewing, and editing the manuscript. He made fundamental and frequent contributions to the essential ideas and their connections to the overall style. The delight I found in our many discussions is one of my principal rewards from this book. Many heartfelt thanks to Roy Tarlow for his helpful suggestions and careful proofreading of the manuscript. I would also like to express my warm appreciation to Jaqueline Ripstein for the beautiful painting which she made for the jacket design.*

# *Table of Contents*

*The approach of the kabbalist to astronomical observations; the contribuition of the Zohar to unlock the cosmic code*

*Is the universe random? The apparent paradox between the kabbalistic view of the order of the universe and that of science.*

*The outlook on the universe as described by Kabbalah; Circles and Straightness; the kabbalist story of Creation; Man's role in Creation; The parallel universes of linear and circular*

*Can the parallel universes one day be harmonized? The view of the Ari and the views of science; knowledge and harmony; the control of mankind over its destiny*

## Chapter 9: Revelation 85

*The meaning of revelation; the Force as a time-machine to remove illusion; the problems connected with the Aquarian Age; the Erav Rav, the Dark Lord; the internal energy-intelligence of evil; the possibility of where the Aquarian Age will lead*

## Chapter 10: Cosmic Influence 97

*Biblical references to celestial bodies; the planets and their influence; the effect on human beings; "to solve our problems"; the comments of scientists and Rabbis*

## Chapter 11: Human control over the Cosmos 109

*The ability of human consciousness to influence the physical nature of the universe; the effect of deeds and actions on our destiny; the effect of Astral influence*

## Chapter 12: Moon Souls 123

*The early kabbalists' observations of the universe inspired by the Zohar and Abraham's "Book of Formation"; Mazal (astral influence)*

### PART THREE
### COSMIC DANGER ZONES

## Chapter 13: Monthly Danger Zones 131

*Monday as a day of negative activity; the fourth day*

# *How*

*did someone,
living some one thousand years ago,
come to possess such knowledge?*

UNTIL THE MID SIXTEENTH CENTURY, COSMOLOGISTS WERE convinced that the Earth was the nerve-center of the universe. The Sun revolved around the flat and perfectly motionless Earth. Demons caused disease. Loons wintered on the Moon. And anyone who had the temerity to suggest otherwise was promptly imprisoned, tortured, and burned at the stake.

In truth, astronomical science was pursued (and in some ways perfected) long before Nicolaus Copernicus at last demonstrated that the Earth, in fact, circles the Sun. Astrologers had for centuries been recording the complex motions of the constellations and were able to make accurate predictions based on their observations. Indeed, at least a few of these early astrologer/astronomers, privileged in their understanding of the unity of the celestial scheme, possessed a vast command of the cosmic forces.

These were the kabbalists.

The early kabbalists' interest in astronomy lay not merely in determining time, seasons, or calendars. They asked *why* does the Earth circle the Sun? What controls astral influences? Where does man fit into the cosmic scheme?

The Italian kabbalist, Shabbatai Donolo (a.d. 913-982) was also a famed physician and astronomer. His precise descriptions of the celestial bodies, their patterns and climatic conditions, in some ways surpass those gleaned from all the NASA space probes and high space technology combined. His knowledge of the heavens, revealed in the *Book of Formation*, is so advanced as to boggle even the most "rational" mind.

How did someone living some one thousand years ago come to possess such knowledge?

To Donolo it seemed clear that if one were to know the heavens it would be necessary to have knowledge of the Ultimate Reality. Obviously, this would require information that lay beyond the confines of our earthly prison, the true barrier to human understanding.

The classic text of Kabbalah, the Zohar (*The Book of Splendor*) provided Donolo and his compatriots with profound insights into the grand cosmological design. Through the study and application of the wisdom revealed in the Zohar, they gained access to the mysteries of interplanetary relationships, including the external movements of the celestial entities, their origins, and the unique internal energies that first motivated them.

From the Zohar,[1] which breaks the biblical code, Donolo and his fellow kabbalists learned many things. They discovered, for example, that everything "below," meaning everything on this the terrestrial plane, corresponds exactly to that which is "above" in the celestial realm. This is the hidden significance of the words:[2] "And the Lord created man in His own image; in the image of the Lord created He him." The Zohar informed them also that on the skin there are shapes and designs — the stars and planets of the body's firmament — through which the wise of heart may behold the hidden mysteries indicated by these shapes and expressed in the human form.[3]

Another method used by the early kabbalists to penetrate the secrets of the cosmos was the study of the Hebrew letters, each of which is imbued with a particular and immense energy-intelligence. When properly understood, the Hebrew alphabet describes how the divine Energy diversified into its various forms, how each energy manifests, the part each plays in the cosmic strategy, and even how each constellation came into being.[4]

Thus, strangely enough, it was through the Zohar, the Hebrew alphabet, and their own bodies, that the early kabbalists penetrated the secrets of the physical universe, while illuminating the origins and deepest esoteric dimensions of the kabbalistic path.

Scientists shake their heads and scoff at such notions — as well they might! For if ideas such as these were ever scientifically validated the majority of scientists would be in the unemployment lines. What need, after all, would there be of space shuttles, if we can travel through space in our minds? What need of satellites, if we can beam our thoughts instantaneously to all parts of the universe? What need of science, if we can learn everything that needs to be known by simply tuning in to the energy of our own bodies?

Fortunately, the kabbalist is not in the least concerned with whether or not the knowledge of Kabbalah will or will not be scientifically verified. What does concern him is personal verification, the kind that can only be achieved through experience. And as any serious practitioner of Kabbalah will tell you, of this (experiential verification) there is no scarcity.

As practiced by the kabbalist, astrology becomes a science of creative living, assuring access to the realm of the Endless, continuity, and experiential certainty. Through the study and careful application of kabbalistic principles, we learn to understand and satisfy our own deepest needs and the needs of those around us.

Unlike conventional astrological wisdom, which contends that man's actions are predetermined by the stars, kabbalistic astrology asserts that the individual is born into an astrological environment best suited for the completion of his or her *tikune*, or cycle of correction. This, however, does not imply any lack of individual freedom of choice. We have many possible futures. If a prior incarnation has destined us for hard times, we can, through the wisdom of Kabbalah, become the captains of our own ships, the masters of our destiny.

Sail on!

# Part One

## The Force, Reality and Future

# 1 The Force

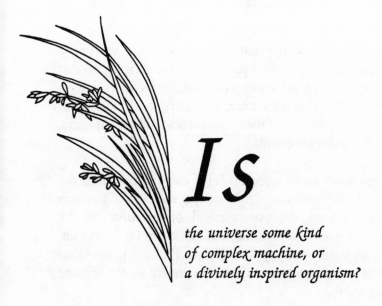

*Is*

*the universe some kind
of complex machine, or
a divinely inspired organism?*

FROM THE BEGINNING OF TIME, MAN HAS SEARCHED FOR possible relationships between the motion of the Sun, the Moon, the planets, and events on Earth. Delve into the works of antiquity and you will find innumerable references, similar in their appreciation of celestial patterns and events. The ancient Greeks, the Mayans, Persians, Egyptians, and Native Americans, to name a few, observed and recorded celestial patterns and events and were able to make predictions according to their observations. Indeed, it was these early recordings of the Moon and Sun cycles that provided later generations of astronomers with calendars, which were gradually improved as the observations from which they were derived were repeated and refined.

Today, many regard astronomy as the most sophisticated of all the sciences. The astronomer, after all, has the profoundly perplexing task of dealing with objects and spaces which are so distant as to seemingly prevent any thought of verifiable scientific experiment. Yet the picture of the origin of our universe as presented by astronomy is vexingly inconclusive — the trouble being that like all the sciences astronomy must limit its investigation solely to the observation of symptoms, appearances and external events.

For the kabbalist there were no false starts concerning the heavens. The classic kabbalistic texts reveal a wealth of modern scientific data. Indeed, the astronomical observations of the world's first true astrologer/astronomer, Abraham the Patriarch, (1800 b.c.), and decoded by the Zohar (70 a.d.), revealed insights that in many ways exceed what is known by the science of astronomy today.

What is of paramount importance to the kabbalist is achieving a thorough internal understanding of the events which motivate actions, both physical and metaphysical. Unlike the astronomer who gazes into the heavens to gather information, the kabbalist gazes at the stars to gain knowledge, knowledge of himself and his place in the cosmic scheme.

As a kabbalist, I have spent many years searching for answers to such questions as *why* does the Earth revolve around the Sun? Where is the source of the drive for this sustained activity coming from?

Early on in my investigation, it occurred to me that the universe knows nothing about the fragmentation or separation subjected to it by the sciences. Thus it seemed that the world, indeed, the entire celestial scheme, would have to somehow be apprehended in its entirety if one were to arrive at a complete understanding of one's place in the cosmic whole.

My search for an answer led me to the Zohar, the classic text of Kabbalah, and the key that unlocks the cosmic code contained in the Bible.

"And Adam knew Eve; and she conceived and bore Cain." [1]

How, the Zohar asks, can the mere act of "knowing" create a pregnancy? The Zohar explains this simply as the difference between information and knowledge. Knowing is the connection. Obviously there was an act of physical intercourse, but that is not the point. The only time information can become connected with us and become knowledge is when we understand and "know" the information intimately. [2]

"And for those persons that do not know, yet have a desire to understand," declares the Zohar, "reflect upon that which is revealed and made manifest (in this world), and you shall know that which is concealed, inasmuch as everything both above (metaphysical) and below (corporeal) is the same. For all that the Lord created in a corporeal way has been patterned after that which is above." [3]

Here we learn the sublime kabbalistic revelation of unseen elements: the concealed will not and cannot conflict with subsequent revealing actions and interactions. [4] Even the most intractable problem can be solved by determining as many facts as possible from observation, and carefully examining these observations to determine if they match the original assumption. This is what is meant by the kabbalistic adage, "Look around you to determine truth."

Astronomy or Kabbalah — which is of greater importance to the individual?

Astronomy gives us quasars, quarks, and black holes. Kabbalah reveals energy, power, and peace of mind. Astronomical investigation leads to more questions, kabbalistic investigation leads to experiential certainty. Astronomy works from the outside in, Kabbalah from the inside out. Astronomy produces apprehension; Kabbalah creates serenity and resolve. Unlike the astronomer who views the universe as some kind of great and complex machine, the kabbalist sees it for what it is, a living, breathing, divinely inspired organism.

I rest my case.

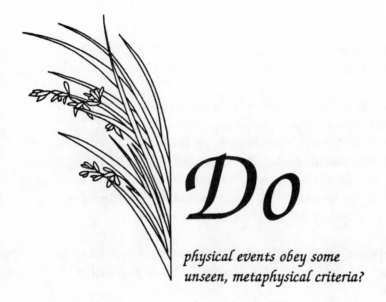

# 2  R a n d o m n e s s

## *Do*

*physical events obey some
unseen, metaphysical criteria?*

DO WE LIVE, AS SCIENTISTS NOW TELL US, IN A CHAOTIC environment, a cosmos that erupted from nothing, without cause or purpose, and which now functions in a purely random way?

Pure disorder or chaos, if it could be found, might be beneficial to the scientist. He might use it, for example, to create a sophisticated code by which banks might prevent thieves from transferring huge sums of money to their own account. Random numbers are essential for secret codes that assure the privacy of bank wire transfers.

Of main concern to the scientist today is the question of whether the universe is random, or if physical events obey some unseen, metaphysical criteria, while only seeming to display randomness. Scientists admit that the fundamental difficulty in seeking true randomness is that while there are many ways to prove that a sequence is not random, there is no way to prove

it is. There is even a lack of agreement among scientists as to
what randomness means.

To the kabbalist's way of thinking, the search for
randomness is an exercise in futility. Had the "Big Bang" been
a random event, such exceptional uniformity as we find
throughout the world would be impossible. A glance at a
snowflake, or a flower, or the vast expanse of space leaves little
question that the universe is a highly structured entity, albeit
one that is engaged in amazingly elaborate activity.

The universe, from a kabbalistic viewpoint, was created in
a divine state of pure order and structure, and so it remains.

The divinely ordered universe was inherent in the Force's
desire to share endlessly of its beneficence. Consequently, the
vessels of Circles were brought into a dynamic interplay with
the Force. And hence the Lurianic definition of the Universe of
Circles expresses the concept of "endlessness," having no
beginning and no end.[1]

How then does one go about reconciling the apparent
paradox between the order of the universe as described
by Kabbalah and the universe of chaos and uncertainty
presented by Quantum Mechanics?[2]

In order to come to terms with this proposition we must
begin by rethinking the myth surrounding problem-solving. The
vast majority of us have been programmed to solve difficulties
through symptomatic or technological intervention. Rather than
solving problems, this approach merely shifts them around,
creating an ever more complex web of human suffering.

Instead of dealing with the problems as they become manifest, the kabbalist asks us to redirect our thinking towards searching for origins and underlying causes.

This is quite the opposite of the way science functions today. Instead of asking why an illness or environmental problem came about in the first place, the scientist studies the symptoms of the disease or outward manifestations of the problem then attempts to interfere with the mechanism.

To assert the idea of "randomness" as truth is to demonstrate an egotistical attitude when addressing inexplicable phenomena. Assuming the scientist could establish some method or definition by which to describe randomness (a large assumption to be sure), he would still be incapable of measuring chaos and disorder. However much data and information one has about the universe, however deep is one's comprehension of the external world, one can never achieve anything but a symptomatic kind of knowledge by studying external appearances. This is like trying to understand a turtle by looking at its shell.

Not only scientists are guilty of symptomatic thinking. World leaders, too, tend to be blind to the origins of conflict and world imbalance and concentrate instead on the external processes. The most severe consequence of this dynamic imbalance is the ever-increasing threat of world destruction, brought about by an overemphasis on self-preservation, self-assertion, and a passion for being right. At the heart of the kabbalistic view of the behavior patterns which dominate humankind and are embodied in our social institutions is the preponderance and dominion of negative energy-intelligence.

According to the ancient kabbalistic wisdom, there are two parallel universes, one highly ordered, the other random and chaotic. The former is real, the latter illusionary. Yet both resulted from a single, clearly comprehensible cause. To achieve a balanced and harmonious integration of these two elements requires that each individual has knowledge of that part of himself which was born into chaos, while at the same time remembering that the greater part of himself belongs to the unified whole. Thus the individual preserves his independence, while at the same time remaining connected with the Supreme Source of his being.

A single all-pervasive Force is the motivation and sustaining influence of all existence, physical and metaphysical, illusionary and real. Only the illusionary aspect of existence behaves in a random fashion. The real aspect, the Force or Endless Light, *Or En Sof*, is constant, eternal, and entirely predictable; for the Light has but one aspiration, and that is to share its endless blessings.

Contrary to appearances, there is no chaos in the universe.

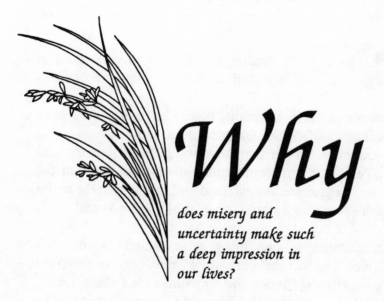

*Why* does misery and uncertainty make such a deep impression in our lives?

FOR CENTURIES PHILOSOPHERS AND THEOLOGIANS HAVE BEEN preaching the need for world harmony. In this century, psychologists, therapists and social workers have taken up the gauntlet, spending centuries in aggregate time and millions of dollars developing techniques for conflict resolution, all to no avail.

If we hope to solve our problems and restore a dynamic balance to the world it will be necessary for each individual to adopt a new outlook on the universe and his or her place in it. Such a perspective is described by Kabbalah.

Rabbi Isaac Luria divided all of existence into two aspects which he called the "phases" of Circles and Straightness.[1] Having no beginning and no end, he chose the circle to symbolize that which is eternal, while the line, being finite, in other words having a beginning, middle, and end, he chose to represent the temporal aspect of existence.

According to Luria, the reality of Circles, unlike the reality of Straightness, suffers no fragmentation. Only the realm of Straightness must endure the pains and pitfalls of chaos and disorder. Perhaps the most important distinction between the two aspects of existence as described by Luria is that the realm of Straightness is an illusion, the realm of Circles is real.

Time, space and motion do not exist within the framework of the Circles. The fact that our rational minds cannot grasp the all-pervasive circular unity in no way limits the holistic reality of which we are speaking. The Light of Circles is here in all its infinite glory, we just don't see it.

Suffering, illness, deprivation, family disruption, these are the trademarks of the realm of Straightness. Doubt, uncertainty and lack of fulfillment are governed by the linear aspect of existence. The world of Straightness, in other words, is the world in which most of us live.

If indeed we live in a perfectly circular universe, why does misery and uncertainty make such a deep impression in our daily lives?

As defined by Kabbalah, the word "creation" is closely tied in with the concept of free will.[2] The creation of the observable physical world, including space and time, permitted man the corporeal expression of the "Desire to Receive for Oneself Alone," which in turn gave us the opportunity of removing what is known to Kabbalah as Bread of Shame.[3]

The kabbalistic story of creation teaches that before the universe was created, we, the vessels, played no role in the cosmic scheme, except as that of receivers of the Force's endless beneficence. This situation produced in us, the as-yet-undifferentiated souls of humanity, shame at receiving something which was not earned. Thus, the Light, whose only desire is to share its endless abundance, but which could not and cannot share unless there is a willing receiver, chose to restrict its endless blessings so that we the vessels might share in the process of creation. That restriction, (known to science as the Big Bang and to kabbalists as *Tsimtsum)* caused an illusionary schism between the Force and the vessels. And so it was that the physical universe was born.[4]

The linear universe came into existence for the express purpose of effecting the role of man as a willing participant in the creative process. However, the universe of Circles underwent no change whatsoever. Certainty, continuity and fulfillment, aspects of the all-embracing reality of the Force, did not disappear. Rather, an illusionary separation occurred between the Light and the vessels, thus permitting the vessels with a way to earn the Light's supreme benevolence. And since that day the only way for the vessels to reunite with the realm of Circles is to pay homage to the first act of creation, which was restriction, and thus lift from our shoulders the burden of Bread of Shame.

Central to the truth as perceived by the ancient kabbalists is the idea of a beautiful and bountiful cosmos, with man in the role of its determinator. With the creation of the illusionary physical reality, man was given the option of choosing when and where and under what conditions he would cause the Light's revealment. This occurred by virtue of the kabbalistic precept of "no coercion in spirituality." For after the *Tsimtsum*, the original restriction, even the Force could not dictate the terms by which we, the vessels, would receive the Light's blessing.

The restriction gave birth to the two motivating principles of the worlds of Straightness and Circles: The Desire to Receive for the Self Alone and Desire to Receive for the Sake of Sharing. If an individual chooses to succumb to the negative aspect of desire, he will remain in darkness. If, however, he takes into account the purpose of creation and its underlying thought process, removal of Bread of Shame, he then achieves an altered state of consciousness which connects him with the parallel universe of the Circles. By reenacting the *Tsimtsum*, the original act of creation, on a personal level, the illusion of randomness, uncertainty, pain, suffering and evil disappears.[5]

What the stage magician accomplishes with his self-confessed illusion, is to reawaken the circular realm of reality, the universe of Circles, which lays dormant in each of us. The idea of two separate and distinct realities is a concept easily grasped by the magician. Not so the scientist.

A central challenge facing scientists today is to explain the expansion of the universe. The kabbalist has established that the expansion of the universe is the result of mankind's increased activity of the negative aspect of desire. The state of universal expansion is illusionary, but illusion was essential to the cosmic process.

Quantum discoveries did not, as physicists believe, prove that our universe is random and uncertain. Quantum Mechanics merely suggests that the individual conscious mind cannot grasp all of reality at once. Despite the fact that the "Circular" universe is scientifically undetectable, scientists continue to pursue a theory of grand unification. Why? Because something tells them that beyond quantum there exists a metaphysical reality, closely aligned with the kabbalistic precept of the Circles.

The Straight or Linear universe emerged as a direct result of the vessels' desire to remove Bread of Shame. The vessel and not the Force initiated the appearance of the Linear universe which includes space and time, randomness and illusion. The Force, in other words, shifted His activity from that of composer to arranger. Henceforth, the music of the universe would depend upon the behavior of man. Viewed from this perspective we see how the entire physical universe becomes the medium of expression of the desire of man.

Thus we speak of parallel universes. One is the linear universe, which is ruled by the negative aspect of desire; the other is the circular universe which is revealed through the positive Desire to Receive for the Sake of Sharing. These two aspects of desire, which are analogous to the positive and negative poles of a magnet, imparted to us free will sufficient to relieve Bread of Shame. At the same time, they shackled us with the inability to see things as they really are.

The Kabbalah reveals the natural laws and principles by which to transcend Bread of Shame and access the divinely ordered universe of the Circles. With the proper attitude of resistance we can pierce the illusion of darkness and bask in Light eternal.

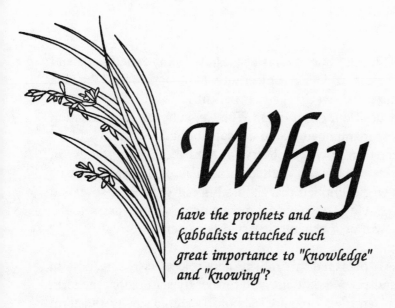

# Why

have the prophets and
kabbalists attached such
great importance to "knowledge"
and "knowing"?

THE ARI, ISAAC LURIA, THE FOUNDER OF LURIANIC KABBALAH, taught that only the linear universe is chaotic and asymmetrical; the parallel circular universe is symmetrical in every way. The metaphysical, circular universe is the picture of absolute perfection, predictable and highly ordered. It is the Garden of Eden, which will one day return to its original pristine splendor.

Can this be? Is it possible that these two seemingly opposing forces, order and chaos, might one day be harmonized?

Three centuries of Newtonian physics has largely succeeded in alienating man from himself and from his environment. Yet there are signs of hope on the horizon. Quantum science is offering new perspectives on what constitutes reality; and astrophysicists, for their part, are rediscovering mankind's intimate link with the cosmos.

In 1927, the famous physicist, Niels Bohr, ended once and for all the classical idea of objectivity. No longer would the idea prevail that the world had a definitive state of existence independent of our observation. The Copenhagen Interpretation of that year maintained that at the subatomic level the world we see depends on how we observe it, and more importantly on what we choose to see. The indeterminism of the subatomic or quantum world implied that the traditional scientist's so-called "objective" view of physical phenomena would have to be replaced by a new observer-created perspective of reality.

The Ari presaged this radical new role of consciousness in physics and even took it one step further by stating that the term "observer" and "participator" should be replaced by the term "determinator."[1]

In his *Gate of Elevated Consciousness*, the Ari describes what must occur when consciousness affects matter: "When a person does a good deed he makes manifest and acquires a personal positive intelligent life force. All essence within our universe has been structured by the actions of man. For even the sound that emanates from striking of a stone by the rod is not in vain. It maintains its rightful place in the cosmos. From even man's word of mouth are created angelic, metaphysical life forces. These very same forces become chariots integrated with the whole of the cosmos. They then connect with the souls of the righteous of the past. Through this interconnectedness, these life form energy-intelligences then serve as providers of cosmic intelligence. They assist the creator (man) of these forces which have become chariots for cosmic intelligences."[2]

Similarly, physicist Jack Sarfatti wrote, "An idea of the utmost significance for the development of psycho-energetic systems is that the structure of matter may not be independent of consciousness."[3]

Spiritual man frequently connects with the all-embracing unified reality. Self-centered individuals, on the other hand, in refusing to let go of the material illusion, experience only the linear universe of chaos and disunity.

When we wake up in the morning, does the same world exist as the one we left yesterday?

Only the external world changes. The real world, the world of circular unity, continues on as it always has, even if we do not perceive it. The conscious mind is a micro-system of the cosmic macro-system, the all-embracing unified reality to which each of us can connect. This universal reality is beyond the space-time-energy-matter continuum. It is the infinite Circle, from which all finite linear life originated, and to which, at the end of the cycle of correction, it will return.

Unlike science which is concerned solely with the "how" of things, Kabbalah is mainly concerned with the "why." It is my deep conviction that only by knowing why the universe acts the way it does, only by knowing intimately the natural laws and root forces of our universe can we begin to truly comprehend life's meaning.

Why is knowledge so essential in comprehending existence? What is the role of knowledge, if any, within the cosmic scenario? Why have the prophets and kabbalists attached such great importance to "knowledge" and "knowing"?

The acquisition of knowledge, is not merely a transfer of information from one source to another. The roots of knowledge run far deeper than the intercourse between teacher and student. More than just a convenient method to achieve a union with the human intellect at the highest levels, the object of "knowing" is to effect a spiritual connection with the cosmic influences and energies of the cosmos.

The path to knowledge lies beyond the realm of the mathematical systems, of quantum, and the physical universe. These are symptoms, false fronts, illusions that hide the true nature of reality. In order to achieve knowledge we must see through the dark veil of illusion that shrouds the material world. With Kabbalah we can lift the veil of darkness and reveal the Light.

A kabbalist maxim reveals that "The thinking process converts knowledge to energy." A verse in Genesis alludes to the intimacy between knowledge and energy when it states, "And Adam knew Eve his wife; and she conceived and bore Cain."[4] In this verse we find the dynamic interplay between knowing and the energy of the sexual union of man and woman. The biblical connotations of knowing and sexual intercourse are inextricably linked.

In nature we find an infinite number of indications that a formative intelligence shaped and structured everything, from a flower, to a man, to a grain of sand. This formative intelligence we call the Force. Millions of people connect with the Force on a daily basis, through prayer, meditation, or with other mental activity. Yet despite the fact that such connections are integral to many lives, the Force remains scientifically undetectable. Nor can the soul, that part of the Force which we carry around inside us, be identified by current scientific means.

The most fundamental natural laws, as well as the most seemingly trivial acts of man, trace back to the heavens and its origins. All forms of energy and life emerged from and are part of the Force. This primal life flow is directed and filtered through many diverse levels of consciousness, thus establishing infinite layers of energy-intelligences. Yet it is but one single all-pervasive energy, expressing itself in an endless multitude of forms and patterns.

In all of creation we find myriad repetitions on a relatively few basic designs. As the atom is one unto itself, structured as the triads in the Shield of David, so too is man, the earth, and the solar system a triad connected as one unto itself. Our universe conforms to the beauty and elegance of this three part atomic harmony.

The Zohar is a book of knowledge and power. The knowledge of Astrology as presented by the Zohar assures all mankind control over our destiny. That control is the astrological connection with the Force. The Zohar[5] states that in the days of the Messianic Age, there will no longer be a need for one to request of his neighbor, "teach me wisdom!" For it is written: "One day they will no longer teach every man his brother, for they shall all know Me, from the youngest to the oldest of them."[6]

According to the Zohar, the day is nearing when the inner secrets of nature will at last be revealed. Such knowledge will enable us to reach the essential life-force which is in us and around us; it will permit us access to the "Circles" domain and provide us with a framework for the comprehension not only of our familiar, observable universe, but of that which lies beyond the range of observation in the realm of the metaphysical.

> For there is not a member of the human body that has no counterpart in the world as a whole. For as man's body consists of members and parts of various ranks, all acting and reacting upon each other so as to form one organism, so does the world at large consist of a hierarchy of created things. When they properly act and react upon each other, they form one organic body. All essences, both of the higher and the lower grades of this world and of the world to come, are to be found there.[7]

What seems to emerge from the Zohar is a revelation regarding the pattern in all structures, from the tiniest atom to the greatest unit of the cosmos. The Force reveals itself in myriad patterns which stem from relatively few archetypal designs.

The main intention of this book is to provide a connection with the chain of intelligence that extends downward from the highest universal level of consciousness to the lesser levels of our terrestrial realm. By connecting our minds with the Force we assure ourselves lives of continuity, certainty, and transcendence of the world of illusions, symptoms and appearances.

Kabbalah can guide us through illusion to the all-embracing reality that the most fundamental natural laws, as well as the most seemingly trivial acts of man, trace back to the heavens and its origins. It is written in the Zohar that Kabbalah would have to await the coming of the Age of Aquarius to make its reappearance as a tool to be wielded by the hands of man as the electronic instrument to draw down the Force upon the human race, which is wandering and confused in cosmic darkness.

That time has come.

*Will*

*we succeed as a
species, or lapse into
extinction?*

AS FAR AS WE CAN DETERMINE, WE ARE THE ONLY SPECIES capable of structuring language and technology. Just how wise we are in our endeavor to communicate with each other is another question entirely. Indeed, how capable we might become in structuring happier, less violent, more productive societies is a topic of vital concern for all mankind.

Will we succeed as a species, or lapse into extinction?

To comment on the future is to risk saying nothing substantial, or worse, to risk being later proved wrong. We all have twenty-twenty hindsight. To predict the future, however, requires abilities which most of us simply do not possess. Or do we?

Perhaps the most compelling argument against prophecy and prediction is the quantum factor. According to quantum science, nature is inherently unpredictable. The science of physics, therefore, has no choice but to pursue a pathway of probabilities. Indeed, since the emergence of quantum mechanics, physics has been relegated to a back seat called the "ability to estimate some probabilities about the future."

Unlike the physicist, the astrologer does not suffer from a plague of uncertainty. Astrology travels the same sure road followed by the celestial bodies. Relying as he does on the predictability of stars and planets, the astrologer charts his course with the same precision as an astronomer, using the celestial beacons to arrive at his destination.

This is quite the opposite of scientists who make wild guesses from one side of their mouths while expressing contempt for the biblical prophecies from the other. The only time the average scientist will turn to the Bible is when he thinks he can "prove" it wrong on grounds of empirical evidence, never realizing that the code contained within the Bible is every bit as empirical as any experiment performed in his laboratory. Yet if these same scientists took the effort to investigate the true, internal meanings of the biblical predictions, they might be in for a pleasant surprise. In addition to gaining a new perspective into the Bible, they might very well come to an understanding of Heisenberg's Uncertainty Principle, which today so confuses them.

Kabbalah holds out the promise of a real science of the future. A valid futurology is indeed possible, this despite the fact that the future appears more complex and unpredictable with every passing moment. As astronomers will testify, there is very little if any indeterminacy in the movements of our celestial neighbors. Astronomy, calendars, and almanacs all rely on what happened in the past to predict the future. These astronomical calculators enjoy wide respect, the simple reason being that unlike the predictions of physicists, economists, weather forecasters, and allopathic physicians, the predictions derived from the celestial movements very often achieve accuracy.

When Einstein revealed his theories of special and general relativity, Newtonian scientists had no choice but to reexamine old familiar and cherished concepts of space and time. Before Einstein's day, time was regarded as a continuous flow, like a river stretching back into the past and ahead into the future. Einstein proved that time is not absolute. Time depends on space, space on time. The two cannot be separated. One cannot be considered without also considering the other.

The famous "twins paradox" is perhaps the most familiar example of this phenomenon. One twin takes a faster-than-light rocket ship into space, while the stay-at-home twin waits for his brother to return some years later. When the space faring brother returns, he finds his earth-bound brother has aged a great deal, while he has not.

A space ship traveling at near light speed would enable such human clocks as heartbeat, brainwaves and blood flow, to slow down during the journey. Time adjusts to accomodate its spacial frame of reference. As bizarre as this sounds, it is true.

In Genesis we find people who lived many hundreds of years: Adam lived 930 years,[1] Methusalech 969.[2] Then, inexplicably, the average lifespan diminished to a low of only 47 years. Now the average lifespan is becoming progressively longer. Could it be that certain ages and civilizations are more conducive than others to achieving non-ordinary states of consciousness?

The dimensions of spacial consciousness as demonstrated by the twins paradox are of course vastly different from those with which we normally deal on the physical level. Yet, this bizarre anomaly pervades every aspect of our daily lives.

Consider the example of two secretaries who, at the end of the working day, may be overheard discussing the day's routine: "The day dragged along," complains one. "I never thought it would end." Her friend, conversely, comments on how swiftly she thought the day went by. Here is an example of how consciousness affects time. The secretary who experienced time in slow motion is likely bored with her job and accomplishes little in the course of her day's work. Feeling down, depressed, unhappy with herself, she has aligned herself with the down side of earth's level, where time moves slowly. The other, meanwhile, gains satisfaction from her work and thus time for her moves swiftly.

Consider another scenario in which two people approach an elevator and both press the down button. After a brief time, one impatiently remarks, "Why doesn't that elevator show up?" The other shrugs and points out the fact that the button to summon it has just been pushed. The former is obviously in a hurry to get where he is going, while the latter who is in no rush does not feel the same pressure as does his companion. Again we see how time varies according to how we perceive it.

With this behind us, we may now begin to understand how the space-time phenomenon makes possible prophecy and prediction. No prophecy was involved in knowing how the two secretaries or the two friends at the elevator would react before the working day was over. By knowing the internal space in which a person exists is sufficient to predict that person's future behavior. The key to prediction is the ability to transcend the bounds of rational consciousness so that we may enter the universal state of mind in which past, present and future exist on the same multidimensional plane.

The astrologer knows well the power of interplanetary relationships and uses them to make predictions. The reason astrologers give so much weight to birthdays is that the birth date provides an insight into the cosmic forces at work at the time of birth. Once an astrological matrix has been established, much of an individual's future can be predicted. Of course the more knowledgeable astrologer will draw upon his intuitive, subconscious level of understanding to provide a more comprehensive map of the subject's journey through life.

To further strengthen the case for astrology, Einstein's Theory of Relativity destroyed the idea of universal time, and of an absolute past, present and future. His imagination led us to believe that in some sense the future already exists. Einstein never did fully explain why universal time no longer exists. After all, to understand the why of things was not then and unfortunately still is not within the province of science.

Uncertainty belongs to the world of physics. In the realm of metaphysics, reality is seen unwinding along a precise, predetermined route that must lead to an unalterable final state. The kabbalist understands that time depends upon a space reference, and there are infinite numbers of space-time references. Indeed, there are as many of them as there are inhabitants of planet Earth.

Our new interpretation of space-time sheds light on the question previously raised as to why people lived long lives closer to the time of the Biblical Adam, and why the average lifespan decreased to a low point only to rise again. Adam and those immediately following him lived in a time of high spiritual consciousness. Consequently, the pressures of existence weighed less heavily on them, time moved slower, and they lived longer. The further removed one is from the rigid framework of clock-time consciousness, the longer one's life is likely to be.

As we approach the Age of Aquarius, our space-time consciousness is being elevated. Time is slowing down for us and we shall experience a marked increase in the human life-span. However, this does not necessarily mean we will all move up to a higher frequency of consiousness. What will take place, however, is a general recognition that past, present and future are no longer fragmented, but are really one and the same.

The biblical parable concerning the Tower of Babel[3] illustrates this point. Although contained in a higher level of consciousness and reaping all the benefits of their state of being, that civilization did not necessarily achieve a spiritual awareness of Desire to Receive for the Sake of Sharing. Because they lived in this upper frame of space-time, however, where fragmented time hardly existed, their grasp of the universe was that of a highly evolved civilization.

Unlike the ancient civilization of Babel, our present civilization will be dominated by the cosmic influence of Aquarius, the essence of which is Desire to Receive for the Sake of Sharing.[4] It is not by chance that the knowledge of

Kabbalah is with each day becoming more widespread and readily available.

As stated in Jeremiah: "And they shall teach no more every man his neighbor, and every man his brother, saying, know the Lord. Rather everyone shall know me, from the smallest to the highest."[5]

Already we are beginning to witness a similarly advanced transition, as did the ancient civilization of Babel. In addition, we are about to experience a spiritual revival, the likes of which did not exist at the time of Babel. No longer is it necessary to accrue vast amounts of knowledge before delving into life's mysteries. In the Age of Aquarius, the ancient wisdom will be the domain of all.

# 6 Prophecy

> But the prophet, that shall speak a word presumptuously in my name, which I have not commanded him to speak; or that shall speak in the name of other gods, that same prophet shall die. And if thou say in thy heart: How shall we know the word which the Lord hath not spoken? When a prophet speaketh in the name of the Lord, if the thing follow not, nor come to pass, that is the thing which the Lord hath not spoken
>
> **Deuteronomy, 18:20-22**

# Who

is a prophet and
how can his validity
be tested?

ISAIAH, IN HIS PROPHECY OF PEACE, SAID, "AND THE WOLF SHALL dwell with the lamb, and the leopard shall lie down with the kid;... for the earth shall be full of knowledge of the Lord, as the waters cover the sea."[1]

Isaiah attributed world peace to the knowledge of the Lord.[2] He had contempt for those irresponsible leaders, intellectuals and planners who create a schism between their own level of understanding and that of the common man. Unfortunately, many scientists have corrupted their pre-eminent position in society by interpreting information according to their own values and attitudes in an attempt to achieve personal gain and self-aggrandizement.

As scientists are quick to point out, the Bible describes many acts which are not based on anything that we today would recognize as scientific evidence. Yet these same scientists who denigrate the ancient prophecies turn around and make similar predictions without batting an eye. Scientists are the first to admit that the world is in imminent danger, that the Greenhouse Effect or a nuclear war might exterminate us, perhaps all life on earth. Yet, in their arrogant view, only they are qualified to make predictions. The biblical prophets, astrologers, indeed, anyone other than themselves who dares to make predictions, they denigrate as charlatans.

How ironic that these selfsame men and women of science, while making their apocalyptic forecasts, never allude to the scriptures, nor do they seem to remember that the principle of uncertainty proved that in the quantum or metaphysical level of existence the scientific method simply does not apply. How, one wonders, can they so blithely dismiss the biblical prophecies when their own theories can so easily be called into question?

As we progress in our understanding of futurism, prophecy, and astrological prediction, we become increasingly drawn to the conclusion that it is the physicist and not the prophet who fills our lives with imminent catastrophe and apocalyptic destruction.

In support of the scientific Doomsday scenario, scientists cite the second law of thermodynamics, which indicates that every day the universe is becoming increasingly chaotic and disordered: people grow old, buildings and bridges fall, shorelines recede, natural resources are depleted, and the seats of our pants are constantly wearing out.

To set the record straight, the prophets and the kabbalists who followed them never claimed to foresee the end of the universe, as scientists do. According to the prophets, mankind can and will survive the apocalypse. If a prophet's vision involved human suffering, he handled it with a great sensitivity and concern as to what could be done to change it. The prophets understood the internal meaning of the Lord's anger, which is a concept that certainly eludes the scientist.

To begin with, there is no such thing in the Lord's universe as reward and punishment. For a definition of this concept consider the electric socket of a lamp in your living room. Screw a light bulb into the socket and you will have the blessing of light; stick your finger into it and you will receive a nasty shock. The results are neither reward nor punishment, but merely the consequence of the individual's action, in his exercise of free will.

Still, millions cling to mistaken connotations of reward and punishment, not because they have proof, but because they think the Bible spells it out. Similarly, millions, Jew and non-Jew alike, refuse even to consider the possibility of astrology.

The tenets of prophecy are founded on the premise that the Lord makes his laws of nature and their consequences known to chosen individuals. The word of the Lord (the Tetragrammaton) is the force by which the balancing mechanism of our universe functions. A prophet is simply one who is endowed with the gift both of receiving and imparting the metaphysical reality.

The prophet is neither a philosopher nor a theologian, but an individual who has achieved elevated space-time consciousness. He is concerned not with the being of the Lord, but rather with the design of the Creator. He reveals the "word" of the Lord to the people, in order to restore and shape a better future by re-forming the present.

Unlike the electric socket experience, in which revelation of its consequence is obvious, the metaphysical realm of the cosmos does very often remain concealed from humankind. Negative activity can wreak havoc because it conflicts with the metaphysical perfection of the world in which we live. There are times when human instinct compels us to act in ways that run contrary to the natural laws of the universe. The prophetic experience thus sometimes seems to reveal a universe of catastrophe and confrontation. But really all the prophet is doing is revealing the dichotomy between the natural perfection of the universe and the negative activity of man.

Divine revelation is delivered by a human agent who is privy to the metaphysical realm.

The prophet is someone with the ability to enter a higher state of consciousness and report to mankind the beauty and dangers inherent in the cosmos and in his (man's) own actions. He is both clairvoyant and capable of predicting future events. Unlike the scientist, the prophet must usually perform the task of bearing the news of divine revelation to an indifferent, if not a hostile, audience.

Consider the medical researcher who, observing a DNA molecule, becomes privy to the future of human eventuality. In a similar manner, the science of astrology provides a fairly accurate picture of what we might call the individual's metaphysical DNA, wherein the individual's past, present and future are grouped together as one unified whole. Such too is the method of the prophet, who enters a multidimensional reality where all things, past present and future, may be seen as one.

The astrologer, like the prophet and the medical researcher, becomes aware of certain predictable events based on the natural laws and principles of the universe. Unlike the prophet, however, neither the astrologer nor the medical researcher must necessarily meet the requirement of an elevated state of consciousness. However any astrologer, or for that matter any scientist, who does achieve an elevated frame of reference will experience a vastly more comprehensive insight when charting the astrological or medical map of an individual than one who remains in a rational frame of mind.

The consciousness attributed to the prophet is clearly described by the Zohar. Though there are several biblical analogues to various prophets, Moses is called a prophet for the first time only in Deuteronomy,[3] which casts him as the prophet *par excellence*. Moses is distinguished by the Lord's direct revelation of Himself.[4] To other prophets, the Lord revealed himself only in visions or dreams.

For an interpretation of this significance, let us turn to the Zohar:[5]

> And Jethro, the father-in-law of Moses took Zipporah, Moses' wife, after he (Moses) had sent her away. And her two sons...[6]

Rabbi Hiyah asked why does the verse state 'her sons' and not 'their sons' or 'his sons'? That is because she cared for them when Moses wasn't there. Rabbi Yosi said that although they were the sons of Moses, the truth, according to the mystical interpretation, is that they were now her sons. Rabbi Elazar stated that because Moses merged with another space-frame, the Shekhinah, they therefore were no longer considered his children. However, when Moses became disengaged from the Shekhinah, and went to meet his father-in-law, the verse then refers to them as his children.[7]

What seems to emerge from this passage of the Zohar is the revelation that different and distinct space-time references may occur at any time. The Zoharic and the Biblical references quoted above are a scriptural testimony of the reality of our spiritual consciousness and our ability to separate consciousness from illusionary reality and to travel apart from all physical manifestations. Through a spontaneous out-of-body experience, Moses was projected beyond physical existence. The spirit and the mind of Moses were capable of changing space-time frequencies and entering into another multidimensional place of existence. Yet, at will, he was able to return with a conscious memory to his corporeal existence in which his children again were his own.

This, then, is the nature of prophecy. A prophet is an individual endowed with a divine gift to disengage from the physical reality and enter the all-embracing reality where one does not experience the limitations thrust upon us by physical time.

Who is to be considered a prophet, and how can his validity be tested?

As a spokesperson for the deity, the prophet's domain lies beyond the finite realm of the fragmented corporeal reality.

They do not choose the profession, but are chosen, sometimes even against their will. The most dramatic example of this is the futile flight of Jonah.[8] Even Moses displayed some reluctance to accept the calling when he exclaimed, "I have never been a man of words... Send I pray thee, by the hand of him whom thou would send."[9]

Moses made several attempts to dissuade the Lord from selecting him, since he felt that he did not possess sufficient wisdom for the mission. He pleaded inadequacy. His level of consciousness was not, he thought, suitable for the weight of prophetic responsibility. His protest of inadequacy was, however, an indication that he was achieving the state of humility so essential to the position of prophecy. Moses' humble occupation, that of a herdsman, was, in essence, the prime reason for the Lord's selection of him.[10]

Thus we find that prophecy is not the hell fire and brimstone preaching that is often described. Prophets are channels who allow us to hear the music of the universe. They are windows that permit the light and knowledge of the cosmos to enter the hearts of all mankind.

# Part Two

## The Cosmic Blueprint

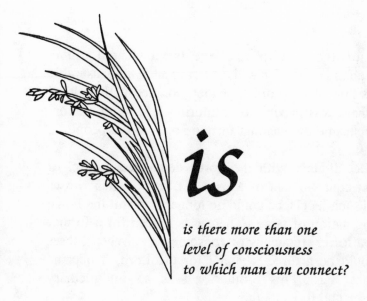

*is*

*is there more than one
level of consciousness
to which man can connect?*

IN THE ZOHAR, RABBI SHIMON BAR YOHAI PRESENTS THE BIBLE
in a light which enables us to reconcile the apparently disparate
elements of the physical and metaphysical worlds. By
understanding the true meaning of the Bible, we can make
connections with the metaphysical world and hidden levels of
consciousness. We thus achieve the pure level of awareness that
we need to "play the strings" of this mundane world in harmony
with the divine music of the spheres.

Prophetic consciousness is rooted in the revelation at Sinai.
The people of Israel were afraid of receiving the Lord's word
directly and they asked Moses to intercede, saying, "Go thou
near, and hear all that the Lord tells you...and we will hear it
and do it."[1] This idea is further substantiated by Moses when he
declares, "I stood between the Lord and you at that time to
transmit the word of the Lord, for you were afraid of the fire
and did not go up to the mountain."[2]

Quite naturally, the people of Israel feared direct communication or connection with power of such immeasurable magnitude as that of the Lord. For they doubted if their level of consciousness was capable of venturing into its dominion. Thus Moses became the channel for the Force to the people.

To connect directly with the Force demanded a level of consciousness equal to that of Moses. At times, when Moses had achieved such levels, he could no longer transmit the Force directly to the nation of Israel. There was a need for a further stepdown to a lower frequency of consciousness. When Moses no longer could be a direct channel for the Lord, it became necessary that Aaron, his brother, act as an intermediary between Moses and the Israelites.

The roles that Moses and Aaron were to assume before Pharaoh are carefully outlined in scriptures: "You (Moses) shall speak to him (Aaron) and put the words in his mouth... and he shall speak for you to the people. And he shall be for you as a spokesman and you shall be for him as *Elokim* (Lord)."[3]

Does this imply that Moses now was replacing the Lord and would serve as the Lord?

Only a superficial understanding of the Bible could bring one to the conclusion that the Tetragrammaton, or the other word, *Elokim*, means or is the name of the Lord. Is the Lord part of some underworld conspiracy that necessitates His using aliases to disguise his true identity? The intent of the Bible in its use of many names for the Lord is to distinguish the various levels of consciousness by which the Force is expressed.

The level of consciousness achieved by a prophet determined which name of the Lord would be implemented. Moses achieved the highest level of spiritual consciousness and consequently the Tetragrammaton level applied to him. The fact that the biblical expression "mouth to mouth" is combined with the Tetragrammaton adds further emphasis to the fact that Moses' level of consciousness was of the highest kind.

This concept is given further credence in the following revealing passage from the Zohar:[4]

And the Lord (*Elokim*) spoke unto Moses...[5] The name *Elokim* hints at justice or judgment. It is written above, "and Moses returned unto the Lord (Tetragrammaton) and said: Lord (Adonai = Aleph Dalet Nun Yod) wherefore has thou in evil entreated this people?"[6] What prophet could speak with such boldness as this Moses? However, from the very beginning of his prophecy he knew that he was destined to a higher level of consciousness. For he was connected to the *Ze'ir Anpin* level of consciousness, which rules and has dominion over the Malkhut level of consciousness referred to in the Bible as Adonai.

Rabbi Isaac said that Moses, who was of an upper level of consciousness addressed Adonai "without fear and trembling, like a steward who has charge over the household."

What seems to emerge from the Zohar is an awareness of the existence of many levels of consciousness to which man can connect. The prophets converged on the scene of human history to assist in balancing cosmic forces, through their ability to connect with and draw upon various layers of consciousness.

The prophet and, to a limited degree, the kabbalist have access to the realm where the separation of past, present and future does not exist.

Negative and corrupt activity by mankind is carried by the channels of cosmos. This negative energy adversely affects the world. Every earthquake, supernova, every war is an expression of violence and hatred in the hearts of men. Contrarily, the positive energy of man creates peace in the world. We have at our fingertips the ability to return to Eden. Instead, we built nuclear warheads and prepare for unspeakable hell.

Thus those biblical prophecies which seem to point to hell fire and doom are nothing more than a prophet's description of consciousness of man. The prophets were merely echoing our choices.

The laws of science are, in reality, laws of probability which enable the scientist to place intelligent bets on the future based on his knowledge of the present state. Unlike Newtonian science, which relates to a very small part of our knowledge of the world, prophecy provides information of the whole physical/spiritual spectrum.

The astrologer is not necessarily a prophet. Just as the physical DNA provides the scientist with a fairly accurate idea as to the future of an individual, so does the cosmic DNA, the astronomical blueprint of the heavens, provide the astrologer with information with which he can determine the future of an individual. With knowledge of Kabbalah, any astrologer can predict with a high degree of accuracy what will happen in any given circumstance.[7] However, the higher the level of the astrologer's consciousness, the more accurate will his forecasts be.

Returning to our question of what constitutes a prophet, the Bible distinguishes between a prophet truly commissioned by the Lord and a false prophet, with the following teaching:

> I will raise them up a prophet from among their brethren like thee (Moses); and I will put My words in his mouth, and he shall speak unto them all that I shall command him.... But the prophet, that shall speak a word presumptuously in My name, which I have not commanded him to speak; or that shall speak in the name of other gods, that same prophet shall die. And if thou say in thy heart: How shall we know the word which the Lord hath not spoken? When a prophet speaketh in the name of the Lord, if the thing follow not nor comes to pass, that is the thing which the Lord hath not spoken.[8]

In another section of Deuteronomy, the Bible goes one step further, explaining that even if a prophet gives oracles that are subsequently confirmed by signs, but should that prophet's message be to worship other gods, that prophet is not to be heeded.[9] Deuteronomy adds a cautionary note to the problem of the false prophet: "Thou shall not hearken unto the words of that prophet, or unto that dreamer of dreams; for the Lord putteth you to a test, to know whether you do love the Lord with all your heart and with all your soul."[10]

Only the future would vindicate the predictions of a prophet. Only when the prophesies came to pass, could it be acknowledged that he who had spoken was a prophet sent by the Lord. But how could anyone pass judgment until history had spoken? To confound matters further, a true prophet might be misled by a "false" prophet.[11] False prophecy might even be inspired by the Lord in order to deceive and entice the people of Israel. The false prophet would have questionable moral character, being in some cases a liar, or drunkard, or perhaps even an adulterer.[12] In some cases, the Lord might actually seduce a bona fide prophet to deliver a false message.[13]

A closer examination of Biblical texts reveals one possible means of distinguishing between the two kinds of prophets. The revelation of "discernment" serves as a tool in assisting mankind in daily existence and in understanding those things that always seem to elude us. Also it must be remembered that the words of the Bible have an esoteric significance. Every word contains hidden seeds of wisdom, comprehensible only to the wise who are familiar with the ways of the Torah. The words of the Bible are not mere dreams — and even dreams have to be interpreted according to certain rules. How much more, then, is it necessary that the words of the Bible be explained in the right way.[14]

A deeper insight of prophecy is required before we can learn not to fall victim to doctrines of illusion and uncertainty. Let us therefore turn to a Zoharic interpretation of the *Book of Genesis* for some dramatic disclosures concerning prophetic revelations.

And Jacob lived in the land of Egypt seventeen years.[15] Rabbi Yosi said that the heart of Jacob prophetically saw in Egypt that his children would endure in many exiles, from then until the coming of the Messiah. And Jacob did achieve the prophetic level of consciousness described by the code word *Vayehi* but only in Egypt. This level of prophetic consciousness had never before been reached by any prophet other than Moses. Jacob and Moses were connected to the upper triad consciousness, whereas all other prophets received their prophetic revelations from the lower triad of awareness.[16]

What emerges from the preceding Zohar is that there are lower and higher realms of prophecy. It was only when Jacob and Moses became enveloped within the dark force of Egypt[17] that they achieved a mastery of and access to the cosmic level where past, present and future are one. Without dominion over the Dark Lord, that is the desire to receive for oneself alone, which was utterly manifest in Egypt, one could not perceive the higher realms of the cosmos. It was therefore essential that Jacob and Moses resided in Egypt before they ascended to the upper triad. Thus we find that an important requisite in determining levels of prophetic consciousness is the degree of mastery over the Desire to Receive for oneself alone. This mastery is the cornerstone and foundation for a true prophet.

Consequently, we now have come to an understanding of the verse previously mentioned concerning the verification of a true prophet.

And if thou say in thine heart, How shall we know the word which the Lord hath not spoken. When a prophet speaketh in the name of the Lord, if the thing follow not, nor come to pass, that is the thing which the Lord hath not spoken, but the prophet hath spoken it presumptuously: thou shalt not be afraid of him.[18]

If the prediction of the prophet dealt with some time in the distant future, how could we in the "here and now" be as certain whether this prophet was credible? The guidelines set down in the Zohar now become invaluable in determining predictability. Does the individual live by the golden rule of restriction and mastery over the Desire to Receive for Oneself Alone? Or does he follow the Desire to Receive for Oneself Alone for the sake of self esteem?

Inasmuch as achieving a higher level of consciousness requires restriction and sharing, the false prophet would immediately expose his incredibility. He would have to, in the opinion of the biblical commentators,[19] reach and achieve a *zaddik* level of consciousness to be considered a prophet.

Dreams, another revealment of future consciousness, have also been instrumental in the prediction of future events. The Bible makes many references to the power of dreams as a vehicle by which to access into the levels of consciousness which transcend the limitations of time, space and motion.[20]

Let us explore the mysteries surrounding the phenomenon known as dreams as recorded in the Zohar.[21]

"And Joseph dreamed a dream..." On the subject of dreams, Rabbi Hiyah discoursed on this text, saying "Hear now my words: if there be a prophet among you, I, the Lord, do make myself known unto him in a vision, I do speak with him in a dream."[22] The Lord has brought into existence a series of grades, one higher than the other, one drawing sustenance from the other, some of the right, others of the left.

The prophets drew their inspiration from upper grades known as vision. The dream, on the other hand, is a mere sixtieth part of prophecy, which is the grade of Gabriel, the supervisor of dreams. Hence there is not a dream that is not intermingled with a mixture of truth and falsehood. Consequently, dreams follow their interpretation, as it is written: "And it came to pass, as he interpreted to us, so it was."[23] In other words, since a dream contains both falsehood and truth, the word (interpreter) has power over it, therefore it is advisable that every dream should be interpreted in a positive rather than a negative manner.

The famous scientist, Sir James Jeans once declared that the universe is nothing but a giant thought. Scientists now suspect that every point in the human brain is connected to every point in the universe. A variation on this idea was expressed by the quantum physicist, Jack Sarfatti, who stated, "signals move through the constantly appearing and disappearing wormhole connections, providing instant communication between all the parts of space. These signals can be likened to pulses of nerve cells of a great cosmic brain that permeates all parts of space."[24]

How does the scientist explain wormholes? They are holes in the quantum foam that connect all regions of space-time. This idea was expressed by the Zohar thousands of years earlier when it states, "one drawing sustenance from the other."

Unlike the rational waking mind, which operates within the narrow confines of space-time, the mind of the dreamer can connect with the collective consciousness, or what Sarfatti called "the great cosmic brain." In dream-time, past, present and future become subordinate to the consciousness of the dreamer, the fabric of physical reality becomes indistinguishable from the fabric of the dream.

The domain of dreams is beyond the physical, illusionary reality. Consequently, the Zohar cautions the dreamer to be careful to whom he reveals his dream, inasmuch as "the word" (the interpreter) has power over it. As the consciousness of the dreamer can generate the dream, so too can the interpreter (the word) generate its subsequent manifestation.

The Zohar, in its familiar style of pressing for ultimate truths, pursues the reasoning that might support the phenomena of dream consciousness.

In a dream, in a vision of the night, when sleep falleth upon men, in slumbering upon the bed; then he openeth the ears of man, and by their chastisement sealeth the decree...[25]

Rabbi Hiyah discoursed on this text, saying: "When a man goes to bed, his soul leaves him and soars aloft. The Lord then reveals to the soul future events. For no revelation comes to man when his body is in full vigour. An angel communicates things to the soul, and the soul transmits them to man."[26]

The body consciousness of man, the five senses, is limited to an apprehension of the physical reality. When man is asleep, the body consciousness control over the soul comes to an end. Unlike the body, the soul is not subject to the space-time paradigm of past, present and future. The soul has access to the quantum consciousness, where past, present and future exist in a single all-inclusive multidimensional plane. The future is for the soul to behold. There is no reason why we shouldn't remember the future as well as the past, since they are equally fixed and invariable, providing we adopt and maintain a correct attitude of restriction.

Gone are the days of astronomers who seek to make fundamental discoveries by merely peering through a telescope. Today, the space scientist relies on physics as an essential tool, by which he hopes to comprehend the origin, evolution and future of all that lies beyond planet Earth. Unfortunately, these types of controlled experiments do little to assist the scientist in his understanding. The problem is that radiation emitted in outer space takes hundreds and thousands of years to reach us here on Earth. Therefore, the scientist sees the universe not as it is, but as it was. This is the penalty for living in a consciousness of space-time.

Kabbalistic astrology does not fall victim to the uncertainties of astrophysics. Astrological data is not conditioned by the observer, nor is it limited to information gleaned from a distant past. More than a tool for prediction, in the hands of a kabbalist astrology becomes an instrument for understanding the karmic pattern in which we are born and the particular forces that compel a person to do whatever he is doing. By understanding the advantages and disadvantages of a particular frame of reference, the astrologer can echo an individual's past, present and future.

# *Why*

*is this age different from any previous one?*

FOR THE ANCIENTS, THE AWESOME BEAUTY OF THE VELVETY black dome of the firmament, studded with twinkling lights, was a main center of attraction. Gazing into the night sky, the more inquisitive observed changing patterns and movements, while a perceptive few began to notice the complex cycles of the stars, the changes in time and position of the rising and setting Sun, the varying shape of the Moon, and a host of other phenomena.

The earliest recorded astronomical observations were made some 3,700 years ago by Abraham, the Patriarch. In his *Book of Formation* we find recognition of the twelve signs of the Zodiac, divided into twelve segments, or signs, at 30 degrees of arc. The twelve arcs correspond to the constellations which describe the outlines of the twelve signs.

For centuries, this astronomical perspective proved to be the guiding light of science. Then along came Isaac Newton, with his remarkably resilient vision of the universe as a perfectly balanced and well-oiled machine.[1] Indeed, until the advent of subatomic physics some three hundred years later, the stronghold of Newtonian science was thought to be impregnable.

Newton's theories ushered in a period of unprecedented industrial development and technological innovation. They brought also the false hope of Progress. Little could Newton have known that in discovering certain seemingly inalienable truths about the physical world he was opening a Pandora's box of psychic and physical ills. The Industrial Revolution gave us many innovations and time-saving devices. But what has it done to our lives?

The by-products of industrial development are, of course, toxic wastes which require disposal. Unfortunately, the only way to eliminate these wastes is to incinerate them, dump them into waterways, or bury them. As a consequence, there is virtually no food or water supply that remains unpolluted. The very technologies we created to make our lives easier and to rid ourselves of diseases are now attacking us through these deadly toxins, which, either by intention or accident, we ourselves introduced into our environment and food supply.

Inasmuch as mankind is completely dependent upon high-technology, no one seems willing to do without the luxuries and perceived necessities it produces. Nor does a decision to turn back the clock and remove technology present itself as a feasible solution. Moreover, very few of us care to assume responsibility, or even to realize the full cumulative affects of our actions.

Another problem facing us today is job-related stress. It seems that for all its apparent glamour, today's business world has generated a harmful atmosphere that burns out bodies and spirits. The psychic climate in many corporations is full of anxiety and paranoia. As tension mounts, blood pressure rises, and that extra drink or two becomes more tempting. If that does not remove the stress, then tranquilizers or other drugs become the alternative. Stress takes a financial as well as a psychic toll on the corporate community. While exact figures are hard to come by, the cost to the economy caused by impaired productivity due to absenteeism and increasing medical costs is estimated to run at a staggering $ 200 billion a year. To all of this add the trauma that ultimately becomes manifest within the family.

As with most crises, entrepreneurs are there to step in and provide instant, if temporary, relief. It is predicted that stress will soon be a $ 20 billion industry. The American Cancer Society has dedicated $ 8 billion to its stress-management programs. Yet medical researchers are still confused about what causes the problem of stress in the first place. Indeed, they even argue over what it is.

It was not so long ago that medical science thought itself capable of detecting and eventually curing most if not all diseases. Yet, despite many advances and improvements in diagnostic technique, the incidence of cancer and other diseases rises at an unprecedented rate.

"Nothing is new under the sun," declared King Solomon.[2] Since the beginning of recorded time, starting with Cain and Abel,[3] self-assertion rather than integration, and competition rather than cooperation, and other causes of stress have been typical traits of all societies. The values, attitudes and behavior patterns which are embedded in our culture were with us long before the advent of Newtonian science. In fact, disease and stress have always been big business, from the days of the witch doctors, right up to present times.

In the patriarchal societies of the past, however, these dangers never appeared as pronounced as they have since we adopted the Newtonian-Einsteinian view of the universe. A good question is why have these problems asserted themselves now, and in a manner that may well bring about the annihilation of the human race?

A clue to the solution of the problems mentioned is provided by the Zohar,[4] in the discourse on the coming of the Messiah.

> Rabbi Shimon raised his hands, wept and said, "Woe unto him who meets with that period. Praiseworthy is the portion of him who encounters and has the divine capacity to be cast in that time".

Rabbi Shimon explained this seemingly paradoxical remark as follows:

> Woe unto him who meets with that period, for when the Force shall make contact with the Shekhinah, (the all-embracing manifestation of the Force), He shall gaze upon those who stand loyal to her, upon all who have become unified with her. The Force shall scrutinize the actions and deeds of each and those who are not found righteous, upon these the scripture declares,[5] "I looked and there is none (Shekhinah) to help." For these, agonizing torment and trouble lie in wait!

Praiseworthy, however, are those who shall merit the joy-giving life Force, those who have become unified with the Shekhinah. Concerning this period "and the evil ones," scriptures state, "I will refine them as silver is refined, I shall cleanse them as gold is cleansed."[6]

Rabbi Shimon confirmed that the Messianic Era will bring with it a Light and a richness representing the infusion of the Force through all the worlds. The dawn of a new world will appear, and with its advent the Force will begin to liberate men from their ignorance, bringing them spiritual awakening and lives of well-being.[7] This objective, declares the Zohar, is inextricably connected with *Hokhmah* (wisdom) and completely dependent upon the dissemination of true knowledge, the sublime wisdom of the Kabbalah.[8]

The Zohar asserts that those individuals searching for a connection with the Force, will be rewarded in the Age of Aquarius with a recognition of the internal relationships between man and the cosmos. With the knowledge of Kabbalah becoming increasingly widespread, a higher consciousness and pure awareness will become the domain of the people.

For every action there is an equal and opposite reaction. This law of science has for centuries been known to kabbalists as the Law of Two Systems.[9] This law permits the removal of Bread of Shame, which is the purpose of creation, and it concurs with the cosmic scheme of free will.

"The Lord has set one opposed to the other," declared King Solomon.[10] From the kabbalistic view, everything, including the celestial bodies have both an internal, positive energy-consciousness and an external, negative energy-consciousness.

This idea follows the general pattern of duality upon which all creation is structured, the physical and metaphysical, the external and the internal, the body and the soul. The body or external consciousness is patterned by the Desire to Receive for the Self Alone. This is the exact opposite of the soul, which, being more closely aligned with the Force, is motivated by the Desire to Receive for the Sake of Sharing.

Our existence, along with that of the cosmos, did not result from some monstrous and meaningless cosmic accident. Only the external aspect of existence is chaotic. The internal state of the cosmos emerged with a high degree of order, coherent and precisely organized, carefully fashioned and extraordinarily uniform. According to the Kabbalah, the universe was programmed to evolve toward a final goal, the completion of a cycle of correction.

If there is a cosmic design and order, where is the evidence that would prove nature's symmetry?

In nature we find an infinite number of indications that a formative intelligence shaped and structured everything in its proper order. The structured order of a universe moving toward an ultimate purpose is evident in the universal compliance of material entities with natural laws and principles. The exploration of the subatomic world in the twentieth century has revealed the dynamic nature of energy and matter. At the quantum level, one observes an interplay within the cosmic web of design and structure.

Recent technological advances have helped scientists uncover many new cosmic phenomena which bring them closer to a Grand Unified Theory, or GUT. Kabbalists will welcome this day, for it will verify what has been known by kabbalists for thousands of years, namely that matter, energy, space and time are manifestations of a ubiquitous all-embracing unified Force.

The Zohar strongly implicates man as the mechanism behind all cosmic activity. It is man who infuses cosmic negative energy into the cosmos which materially makes manifest the energy-intelligence of chaos and disorder.

With the coming of the Age of Aquarius people will be given the choice of fulfilling the purpose of creation, thereby vaporizing the negative intelligence within the cosmos, or succumbing to the negative "Desire to Receive for Oneself Alone,"[11] thus permitting the rulership of the evil over the entire cosmos.

Observe, that when the days of man are firmly established in the supernal celestial grades, then man has a permanent place in the world. However, if man has not taken his rightful place in the cosmos of the outer space connection,[12] his days descend until they reach the cosmic level where the Dark Lord resides. The Angel of Death then receives authority to take away man's soul, polluting his body so that he permanently remains part of the dark side.

Happy are the righteous who have not polluted themselves and in whom no pollution has remained.[13]

Kabbalists say that the thinking process converts knowledge to energy. Many people communicate with the Force on a daily basis through prayer, meditation, or other mental activity. Yet despite the fact that it is an integral aspect in the majority of human lives, the Force is scientifically undetectable. Nor can the soul, that part of the Force which we carry around inside us, be identified by current scientific means.

Does this in any way imply that the Force does not exist? Of course not. It means only that the scientific method is an inadequate way of detecting its existence.

Although, from our limited perspective, the two worlds of spirit and material substance seem to be two distinct and separate entities, there is no reason why they must remain so. They can be integrated by the thoughts of man.

The early kabbalists sensed and had a firm conceptual understanding of the unimaginable abyss of time and creation. However, having no language by which to share with the world their intuitively gleaned truths, they passed on their knowledge in secret, by word of mouth, from one generation of kabbalists to the next. During the intervening centuries it seemed as though the truths of the Kabbalah, at least for the layperson, might be "closed up and sealed till the end of time."

Those who pollute the cosmos with their negative activity live in a world of friction, decay and destruction. For them life's secrets are indeed sealed, locked in a vault of ignorance and misunderstanding.

Woe unto them, for they are removed from the Force and distant from Him. The upper and lower dimensions of energy-intelligence abandon them and they no longer participate in the living interplay of things.[14]

The Zohar identifies the Age of Aquarius as the opportunity for man to enjoy a sense of heightened awareness not known since the days of the Temple. He will have the power to tap the eternal circular reality, the realm of certainty, and draw this energy-intelligence into the sphere of his own existence. Thus he will infuse his daily life with positive energy-intelligence to assist and support his mental and physical well-being.

The Bread of Shame dictum decreed that man surely could and would have the ability to influence the cosmic order. In the Age of Aquarius man will again return to his proper and rightful role in the cosmic unfoldment. Elevated awareness is available to anyone who makes use of the Kabbalah, (the cosmic code of the universe). Armed and equipped with the Aquarian revelation, man can again assume his position as Emperor within the cosmos.

# *What*

*is the phenomenon
of revelation?*

TIME SEEMS TO BE MOVING AT AN EVER-INCREASING RATE OF speed. In an amazingly short span of time we have developed from the day of the horse and buggy to an era of space travel. Fiber optics have replaced cumbersome cables. Lasers perform surgery with minimum intrusion. Whole cities can be destroyed with the push of a button. More is less; less is more.

To what might we attribute this phenomenal change in our environment?

According to the Zohar, "All the celestial treasures and hidden mysteries which were not revealed to succeeding generations will be revealed in the Age of Aquarius."[1] It is said that the new age will provide us with a comprehension not only of our familiar universe, but of that which lies beyond the range of observation in the realm of the metaphysical, the non-space domain. We are seeing the beginning of a new age of revelation. Today, more than at any other time in history the Force is demanding to be revealed.

"As the Force separated those on Mount Sinai, so shall He separate them at the final redemption."[2] The Revelation on Mount Sinai is interpreted by the Zohar to mean a connection between the raw energy of the Force and the nation of Israel. Hence, the use of the word "revelation" which means being revealed without the usual protective elements that cloak and conceal. The Aquarian Age, then, will be an age of revelation.

With the removal of the illusionary, corporeal realm of reality, the Light on Mount Sinai was revealed in all its glory and the collective consciousness known as the nation of Israel was greatly elevated to one of unity with the Force.

Rabbi Shimon said that when the Lord, the Force, revealed Himself on Mount Sinai, He called together His whole celestial family and told them that at present the Israelites were like little children; they did not know how to deal with His presence (the naked reality of the Force). If He would reveal Himself to them in the attribute of Power (raw, naked energy), they would not be able to bear it. He would therefore manifest Himself to them as *Rahamim* (compassion).[3] Therefore the revelation of Mount Sinai took place on the third day,[4] which is the day of *Rahamim*. He then gave them the Torah from the side of Power, (*Gevurah*: raw, naked energy). Three is the meaning and concept known as Israel.[5]

Religion, as it is widely practiced, does little to alleviate the problems of daily life. The vast majority of Christians and Jews derive scant benefit from the biblical precepts. Routine religious observances do little or nothing towards the elimination of man's inhumanity to man. Given this, it stands to reason that religion is thought by many to represent nothing more than a stifling impediment toward the enrichment of one's goals and ideals.

The purpose of the Bible is not to tyrannically regulate behavior. When understood from a kabbalistic perspective, the Bible brings meaning to life by revealing and eliciting the beauty and power of creation. The biblical code, combined with methodical meditation, stimulates the harmonious movement of pure thought-intelligence, resulting in a lingering sensation that one has been listening to the most exquisite musical harmonies.

Reflecting on the verse, "And all the people saw the voices..."[6] the Zohar raises the question as to how one can "see" voices. Surely it ought to be "heard the voices." No, we have been taught that the voices were created from the threefold elements of darkness, so that they could be visibly apprehended. Because they were bathed with the supernal light of the Force, the Israelites of the exodus generation perceived things that others before and after them did not. They all came "face to face" with the Force, without fear of being burned by its naked energy.

The words of the Zohar, "face to face," describe a universe where all manifestations, physical and metaphysical, can be tied together in a web of interconnected relationships, each apart from and yet part of the unified whole. This same idea is expressed in the Bible when it declares, "Face to Face spoke the

Lord."[7] And what did they see? According to Rabbi Jose, from the energy-intelligence of these voices came a perception of all hidden things.

The generation of the Exodus even saw all the future generations of mankind up to the days of King Messiah.[8] The startling declaration by the Zohar reveals that events can operate not only from the past to the future, but also from the future to the past. The Force is our time machine, our entrance to the higher worlds. Only the Force is capable of removing the illusion of corporeal reality, revealing a cosmic model that is, was, and will always be, timeless and full of certainty. This was the phenomenon of Revelation.

It was Moses, on Mount Sinai, who transformed a horde of slaves into a nation with the potential ability of securing peace and harmony in the world. However, when Israel fell under the influence of the Golden Calf,[9] its connection with the Force ended. The Israelites could no longer harness the awesome power of the Force and eventually perished in the wilderness. This event occurred simply because they let their level of spirituality descend and therefore became the natural victims of suffering, through the subsequent centuries of diaspora, persecution, and eventually the nightmare of the holocaust.

Revelation was an opportunity to connect with the proper tools and channels for achieving an altered state of consciousness that enabled Moses to connect with the Force. The Force was revealed. There was no turning back. But the awesome power of the Force was too much for mankind to handle.

Throughout the Zohar, there are many references to the dark period and concept of Armageddon.[10] In my book, *Star Connection*,[11] I made reference to cosmic upheaval and its connection with the actions of humankind. The scriptural descriptions indicate a link between chaos and human activity. But why connect the gloom of Armageddon to the Aquarian Age?

The Ari, Rabbi Isaac Luria, considered the problems connected with the Aquarian Age and provided an insight into the root of this matter, which he derived from the doctrines of reincarnation.

According to the Ari, the Israelites that were given the revelation on Mount Sinai, were incarnated with souls of the highest intensity of the "Desire to Receive." This was to enable the Force to infuse the cosmos with Endless Light and beneficence. To avoid catastrophic short-circuitry, the Revelation of the Mosaic Law, including the 613 precepts, was necessary to insure that humanity could achieve and demonstrate restriction, the energy-intelligence of the "third column."

The Noahide Laws were insufficient to curtail the degree of the Israelite's "Desire to Receive." Only the biblical system of restraint was capable of achieving the fulfillment of man's task in this world if his soul became incarnated as a Jew.

The souls of the *Erev Rav*[12] at the time of the Exodus displayed an arrogance and insensitivity that assured the failure of their mission. Even today, persons lacking compassion, sensitivity, and tolerance for others corrupt the cosmos with their negative energy-intelligence. It is to them that we owe a world torn by violence. They are directly responsible for holocaust and destruction throughout the world. In this connection, a good starting point for an understanding of the *Erev Rav* is to refer to the Zohar, which places emphasis on the consciousness of these people.

There are five groups within the *Erev Rav.* These represent five groups of evil people in the world. The third group, known as *Geborim,* are the builders who are assimilated amongst the Israelites. They are incarnated souls from the generation of the Tower of Babel.[13] The builders of edifices, they construct places of worship and houses of study. They dedicate scrolls of the Torah and put crowns upon the scrolls. However, their acts are anything but altruistic. Their one purpose is to create an image and name for themselves. As it is written, "let us make for ourselves a name."[14] These individuals are boisterous and vocal and dominate those who have been blessed. Ultimately their selfish indulgence causes their places of worship and houses of study to be broken and destroyed.[15]

Throughout the Bible, we read of a nation never ceasing to be dissatisfied, ever complaining and never recalling the good that the Force had provided for them. The *Erev Rav* were responsible for the making of the Golden Calf.[16] When again, as many times before, "the *Erev Rav* that was amongst them felt a lust, they wept again, and said, 'who shall give us flesh to eat? But now our soul is dried away?'"[17]

Moses brought them into the nation of Israel and he pleaded on their behalf for the purpose of cleansing and elevating this evil consciousness so as to make it do only good. But even

Moses finally lost his patience when he realized these kinds of Jews were beyond salvation. His remarks indicated his despair when he pleaded with the Lord: "Why hast thou afflicted thy servant? I am not able to bear all this people alone, because it is too heavy for me."[18]

The *Erev Rav* were granted freedom,[19] the miracles of the ten plagues, the splitting of the Red Sea, the miracle of the Manna.[20] And all they could think of was, What, Lord, have you done for us lately? Their ingratitude, arrogance and insensitivity prompted the Lord to declare an end to them.

> For all these people who saw my honor, my miracles
> that I did in Egypt and in the wilderness, they have
> proved me ten times and still do not harken to my voice.
> If they shall see the land that I promised to their
> forefathers, all those that scorn me shall not see that
> land.[21]

The Erev Rav were incapable of completing their *Tikkune* in their then existing corporeal bodies. Having no choice, the Lord decreed, "Your carcasses shall fall in this wilderness and all that were numbered of you, according to your whole number, from twenty years old and over, which have murmured against me."[22]

In this connection, the verse for the very first time attaches the word "Nazi"[23] to the evil consciousness of the Jew; a most startling declaration, in light of the recent holocaust in which the perpetrators of mass murder, torture and terrorism were also known as Nazis.

Throughout recorded history, humankind has been divided into two basic categories, the Israelites and the *Erev Rav*. The bloodstained history of religious conflict incorporates these two qualities. All religions are made up of those who accept the premise of "Love thy neighbor," and those who purvey the energy-intelligence of evil. Intolerance, prejudice, and bigotry in the name of the Lord are manifestations of the antisocial face of the Dark Lord, the Erev Rav.

When governments or religious organizations sanction torture (physical or evil tongue), suppression, and genocide, the internal energy-intelligence of evil becomes physically expressed within the cosmos and that segment of humankind that is not necessarily evil, but on the borderline between good and evil, is impelled to resort to negative activity. Even good people can get coerced into performing negative acts and accept a continuity of evil, despite their basic intuition of positiveness.

The editor of Newsweek magazine, laying out his weekly edition, once hit upon the idea of a front page clock with its two hands marking the hours of 5 P.M. and 7 P.M. These were the hours when most crimes throughout the world were committed. What the editor failed to question was why these hours were impelling criminals to perform their acts.

Was there some universal convention of criminals in which a decision was made to choose these particular hours? Hardly! In fact, there is a period near the time of sunset when negativity is visited upon all mankind.[24] Sunset itself is not the cause of criminal activity; this distinction goes to the astral influence that brought about sunset. It is at this time that an individual with a negative tendency might be prodded into criminal action.

From the kabbalistic viewpoint, celestial bodies reflect an internal cosmic intelligence that compels them to follow a particular path. The kabbalist is not primarily concerned with the physical aspect of the Earth's rotation or its journey around the Sun. The kabbalist asks what cosmic force creates a particular physical expression.

From the inner working of the atom, to the complex surrealism of human behavior, Rabbi Isaac Luria's radical kabbalistic interpretations reveal the fundamental laws that govern the behavior of cosmic forces. Lurianic Kabbalah enables us to comprehend some of nature's most closely guarded secrets. Central to this approach is an understanding of the basic doctrines of reincarnation.

> The generation of *Dor-Deah*, the exodus generation,
> the generation of intelligence, shall once again rise in
> reincarnated souls during the Age of Aquarius.[25]

Here the Ari demonstrates his familiarity with the internal cosmic activity and intelligence of the Aquarian age. The *Erev Rav*, who are reincarnated from the Dor-Deah, will be at the forefront of this evil manifestation.

Man will be the determining factor as to where the Aquarian Age will lead. Will the evil energy of the *Erev Rav* be harnessed for peaceful purposes, leading us to a cosmos of interdependency and inseparableness, or will they fail the golden potential of the age by insisting on continuing with their arrogance, and thus continue a world of cruelty and intolerance towards their fellow man?

If the *Erev Rav* consciousness is permitted to reign, havoc will infuse the cosmos. Should this happen, the Age of Aquarius will usher in an avalanche of deepened hatred and hostility which will fester all over the world. Hence, the Zohar's declaration, "Woe unto those who shall be present in that time."

If, however, the human soul is prepared for the renaissance of Messiah, the consciousness of "Love thy neighbor" will deliver all peoples from exile. "And men shall dwell in it, and there shall be no more utter destruction,"[26] states the scripture. The solution is contained within the revelation, "Love Thy Neighbor." Thus, comments the Zohar, "Praiseworthy are those who shall be present in that time."

Attention must be directed to our ability to differentiate between those souls originating from the positive energy-intelligence and those of the *Erev Rav*.

As long as the balance of power depends upon human activity, the *Erev Rav* represent a threat to cosmic and world stability. Indeed, already in our time, the cosmic arena is turning into an energy-intelligence struggle between the forces of good and evil, adding dangerous complexities to the already precarious balance of terror, drug-warfare and crime.

Who are the *Erev Rav*? The question is answered by the Ari, Rabbi Isaac Luria: "And these are the *Erev Rav*, those who contemplate, ponder, and have thoughts of evil, negative intelligences."[27] The *Erev Rav*, by means of their corrupt deeds, place evil in a position to seize the power of the Force. These malevolent individuals, in whatever religion or incarnation, fill the world with chaos and turbulence.

Sociologists and government planners express deep concern about our inability to respond to the breakdown of family traditions. Time-proven values which have been supportive of relationships, are crumbling and becoming meaningless to our society as a whole. The increase in correctional facilities and mental institutions, and the acceleration of medical illness, all point to the negative aspect of the Aquarian Age and the influence of the *Erev Rav*.

In this the Aquarian Age, we will all be infused with the insight to guide us through illusion to the ultimate, all-embracing reality, the Force. Knowledge of the Force will be the dominion of all. Should we choose to use this knowledge in the service of good, we will return to the Garden of Eden; should we use it in the service of evil, we will bring to our lives the energy of Armageddon.

Which do you choose?

# Do

*celestial forces
exert an influence
on us and our planet
earth?*

EAST VERSUS WEST, POLITICAL CONFLICT, RELIGIOUS AND political leaders falling from grace, gangs, drugs, wars raging all over the world — if only we could get away from it all!

The night sky remains a wonderful channel of escape from the cares and worries of the world. Many of us turn to the starry cosmos as therapy when we suffer some form of trauma or anxiety.

Have you ever found yourself lying on the grass on a warm summer night, staring up at a clear star-lit sky? As we smell the sweet fragrance of the summer foliage and gaze at the distant stars, we are whisked away from our mundane concerns. At such times, it is easy to abandon ourselves to the incredible beauty of the cluster-filled panorama of the heavens and enter a state of deep relaxation.

A gaze into the night sky instills us with a new perspective on everything. With nothing around to steal our attention, nobody to remind us of our worldly problems, we begin to see things in their broader cosmic context, and truly feel connected with the whole universe.

We all respond to planetary action, for better or for worse. The responses of human beings to planetary stimuli is a truly amazing phenomenon. No wonder we "thank our lucky stars" for our moments of good fortune. On some deep internal level we know that our destiny and happiness are somehow bound up with and connected to the stars.

Yet sensing our connection with the universe does not enable us to deal with the difficulties of our planet once we have returned to everyday reality. On our return to mundane existence we again find it difficult if not impossible to solve the riddle of our lives, much less face the problems of the world. As if by inescapable instinct, we turn to others for solutions to our perplexities. We seek happiness outside ourselves, whether in love, religion, government or science. In fact, the key to the star connection rests within.

Every race and nation — Egyptian, Chinese, Persian, Babylonian, to mention a few — include in their history the teachings of astrology.

Despite attacks from many sources, the oldest of all sciences, astrology is today more popular than at any time in history. Kabbalistic Astrology addresses the causes of human conduct, as well as providing explanations for celestial activity.

Its roots were planted four thousand years ago, in the ancient and first known work on the Kabbalah, *The Book of Formation*, authored by the Patriarch Abraham.

Several parts of the Bible, once decodified, confirm the existence of astral influences.

> And the Lord made two great lights; the greater light to rule the day, and the lesser light to rule the night, He made the stars also.... And to rule over the day and the night, and to divide the light from the darkness.... And there was evening and morning, Day Four.[1]

By the words "to rule," the Bible means to manifest or to dominate. The sun and the moon, referred to in the foregoing verse, are cited as "ruling" bodies.

Both the Bible and the Zohar make it abundantly clear that "chance" does not answer the question of why things happen to us. There are some bizarre coincidences — inspired events — which only astrology can explain. But what kabbalists have always known, and what a growing number of scientists are beginning to realize, is that man is a vital and responsive element in the cosmos, even if the forces that dictate to man remain largely unseen and unknown.

Early kabbalists were familiar with the internal cosmic fields of celestial bodies and regarded each constellation and planet as an intelligent entity in which the constant forces of the four elements, water, fire, air, and earth, were operative. Their observations of the universe, drawn from the various source reflections of the Zohar, enabled them to provide a valid guide for the individual in his search for a total understanding. More importantly, they provided a discipline which had the ability to elevate the individual to a higher level of consciousness and moral conduct.

The Sun and Moon exert the most direct influence over Earth's inhabitants, followed by Saturn, Jupiter, Mars, Venus and Mercury. It is noteworthy that according to kabbalistic astrology all astral influences are based on the cosmic energy centers of these seven planets. They are the only channels for directing the power of the cosmos. The other three planets, Pluto, Neptune, Uranus have no direct influence.

The majority of the Talmudic sages believed in and understood the decisive role played by celestial bodies in determining human affairs. While they conceded the possibility that astrologers might well be able to predict the future by consulting the stars, the sages claimed that the majority of astrologers failed to understand the contents of their forecasts.

Astrology and Kabbalah today enjoy an enormous popularity in the public mind. However, both disciplines, as they are popularly conveyed, are rife with myth and misconceptions. The Zohar I am about to quote may offend some astrologers, even though I do not necessarily find a contradiction between the Zohar and conventional astrology.

"And the wisdom of their words was lost, for the wisdom of their wise men shall perish and the understanding of their prudent men shall be hid."[2] The words "was lost" refers to the wisdom of the ancient Egyptian astrologers whose internal understanding was and is concealed from them.[3] This is because, as the Zohar goes on to explain, "...they do not know the initial creation of the celestial bodies, but only their manifest uses. Their knowledge is based on the changes that are observed in the world they experience, in their travels, and in the way they are made use of."

In other words, the ancient Egyptian's philosophy of astrology was not founded on the internal structure of creation, meaning the original cause for the physical manifestation of celestial bodies. From the kabbalistic viewpoint, the cyclic pattern of a celestial body is a reflection of an internal cosmic intelligence which compels it to move in its particular path.

Like the celestial bodies, man, too, moves according to both external and internal influences. Within the overall composite of the human being we find two basic elements, or energy forces, that propel him into action: the metaphysical and the physical, the external body and the internal soul. The body conforms to its basic tendency which is a desire to receive for oneself alone, whereas the soul's essence exists for the purpose of imparting. The soul expresses the positive polarity of consciousness, the body expresses the negative polarity.

This duality of intelligent consciousness exists both in the celestial and terrestrial realms. Whether it be the body of a man or the body of a planet, the external aspect is dominated by the negative energy-intelligence, which reigns over chaos and disorder, while the metaphysical internal aspect is ruled by the positive energy-intelligence, whose domain is timeless, all-pervasive, and irrefutably certain.

The objective of this work is to help the reader tap the internal, positive power of the cosmos, while at the same time avoiding the traps set for us by the external, negative influence.

The biblical account of the Creation is understood by kabbalists to mean the creation of the positive and negative energy-intelligences, the Desire to Receive and the Desire to Share. The creation of the observable physical world, including man and the planets, permitted mankind to be influenced by corporeal expressions of the Desire to Receive for the Self Alone. The two opposing desires accomplished to give the human race the opportunity of removing Bread of Shame through the process of Restriction.[4]

Can something happen without any prior action, or rational reason? Science, with the new phenomena of quantum, has been making strong statements challenging the claim that every event has a cause. In its search to prove false the assertion that every event has a cause, science not only would have to find an event for which no cause existed, it would also have to demonstrate a total understanding of nature. Otherwise, how could one ever be certain that the event in question is not caused by some totally obscure, never before encountered creative process?

Consider, for example, a situation is which an unwitting motorist is driving on a highway at the exact moment that a drunken driver crashes through a guard-rail causing a head-on collision. No matter how much information is available about the two drivers and their cars, there is no scientific way to determine how both drivers happened to arrive at the point of impact at the same time. The outcome is thus considered intrinsically random and unpredictable.

Another example of the random dilemma is the problem of illness. Cancer, an abnormal and unrestrained new growth in the cells and tissues, is potential within all of us. Normal cells and tissues are considered cancerous, when, for no known reason, they cease functioning in a normal manner. Why does cancer strike some and not others?

The Talmudic sages believed in the decisive role played by celestial bodies in determining human affairs. All of civilization is bound up and connects with the movement and influence of the cosmos. Each "unknowable" event can be traced to some aspect of celestial intervention, and that includes the mishap with a drunken driver, as well as the beginning of an illness.

In several places in the Talmud it is stated that every man has a celestial body — a particular cosmic influence which is his master from conception and birth.[5] Even inanimate objects are not free from astral influences. The Bible is replete with references to invasions of inanimate objects.[6] Stars in certain constellations were connected with the growth and ripening of the fruits.[7]

While there is no explicit mention of astrology in the Bible, most, if not all of its contents are revealed in stories, narrations and precepts unquestionably linked with astral influences.

The Jewish New Year, or the first and second day of the Hebrew month of Tishrei, determines the life or death of all humankind.

> Rabbi Elazar said: "This day is called 'the concealing for the day of our feast,'[8] because the moon is still covered and does not shine. On this day the moon is covered and it does not shine until the tenth day."[9]

The Zohar clearly defines the cosmic position of the moon on the first day of Tishrei. The life sustenance of all humankind is

withheld from mankind for a full ten days. This is the awesome
negative state of cosmic domination by which life on planet
Earth becomes threatened with extinction.

The Talmud extends this idea by declaring that not only
human beings are influenced by the stars, but that there is "not
a blade of grass that has not its star in the heavens to strike it
and say to it: grow."[10]

It is not insignificant that experts in many fields can no
longer deal with problems that arise in the area of their
expertise. Physicists are baffled as to the structure of matter;
police are helpless in the face of rising crime; oncologists are
totally confused about the causes of cancer; and psychiatrists
are in a state of confusion as to the cause of mental illness.

Despite the many advances of scientific medicine, and
continuing claims of medical excellence, the health of the world
population does not seem to have improved significantly. The
mechanistic view of the human organism and the resulting
scientific approach to health with its excessive emphasis on
medical technology has apparently produced few lasting positive
results.

To solve our problems will require nothing less than a
spiritual revolution. We must adopt a dynamic and
revolutionary new world view, with awareness of the profound
connection between crisis, good fortune, and the cosmos.
Several social indicators already point in this direction. The
rising appeal of astrology, the general sense of dissatisfaction
with the status quo, the search for a greater awareness of our
existence, the interest in altered states of consciousness, the
increase in holistic medicine, all of these indicators provide

evidence that we are indeed on the verge of spiritual upheaval such as the world has never known.

The famous quantum physicist, Niels Bohr, once wrote, "isolated material particles are abstractions, their properties being definable and observable only through their interaction with other systems."[11] The skeptic with doubts about the wisdom of astrology might consider the subatomic realm, where nature manifests as a complex web of relationships between the various parts of a unified whole. In the light of such evidence, he would be wise to let down his defenses and accept the reality and totality of the cosmic plan.

A number of the sages of the *Mishnah* (Tannaim), such as Rabbi Akiva[12] and Rabbi Johanan seemed to indicate that the power of the stars did not extend to the people of Israel. Rabbi Johanan said, "there is no star, no sign of the constellation for Israel."[13] Contrarily, Rabbi Hanina ben Hama stated "The stars make one wise, the stars make one rich, and there are stars for Israel."[14] Mar Samuel, who was an astrologer and an astronomer, aligned himself with those who maintained that the stars do indeed influence the people of Israel, by formulating several guidelines of agriculture and health founded on astrological principles.[15]

On the surface it might appear that the rabbis were divided as to whether the people of Israel were influenced by the power of the stars. Certainly, the authority of Rabbi Akiva should have been sufficient to dissuade other sages from opposing his views on astrology. Rabbi Akiva's acknowledgement that the stars do indeed influence the people of Israel was indicated by the credence he gave the interpretation of astrologers with regard to his own daughter.[16]

Rabbi Akiva was told that his daughter was destined to die on her wedding night. Rabbi Akiva knew that the past, present and future were somehow linked and was uncertain whether his daughter could overcome the impelling interpretation of the stars that had sentenced her to die on the night of her wedding. This precognition was a continuing source of pain for Rabbi Akiva, up to and including the night of his daughter's marriage.

Although Rabbi Akiva knew and advocated the science of astrology, he did not feel that the stars dictated entirely over the actions of man. It was his opinion that "righteousness delivers from death,"[17] which is just what happened, in spite of the grim astrological forecast.

As it turned out, Rabbi Akiva's daughter was spared because she resisted her normal inclination to pay attention to the wedding guests. Instead, she personally saw to it that the poor were attended to, and was delivered from death by the positive energy generated by this selfless act.

As to the question of whether or not the stars exert influence on the nation of Israel, we find that the sages were expressing two perspectives on the same reality. Rabbi Akiva presented the idea that while the stars impel, they do not compel. He acknowledged the impelling character of celestial bodies, yet he knew how to rise above their influence. He therefore concluded that there are no stars for Israel. The other sages also realized that the stars influence man's behavior, but did not direct their attention to man's ability to control the astral powers. They did, however, agree to the possibility that the influence of the stars would not extend to Israel when Israel has mastered the science of cosmic control.

As the kabbalists before us, many today are becoming intimately informed of the impelling influence of the celestial energies. The Zohar tells us how these forces present themselves in the universe, and how they may be controlled.[18]

# Can

*human beings exercise
control over cosmic influences?*

FROM THE NEWTONIAN PERSPECTIVE, HUMAN BEINGS WERE SEEN
as little more than complex machines, involuntarily caught up
in a mammoth mechanistic universe. The new physics, with its
uncertainty principle, makes a strong case for free will, while
endowing the individual with an important role in the nature of
physical reality, but it neglects man's spiritual side. With the
know-how of Kabbalah, we can integrate free will and
determinism and achieve a status not unlike the one enjoyed by
Adam before "the sin."

We all take for granted that the sun will set in the west and
rise in the east the next morning. We plan our summer vacations
during the wintertime. All seasonal clothing is designed and
manufactured based on the premise of a future season that has
not yet arrived. Retirement villages come into existence as a
result of knowing future climatic conditions. These are just a
few of the myriad indications of how cosmic determinism

influences the way we live. It should come as no surprise that determinism is injected by the cosmos into areas that are not so easily seen.

In at least one respect, the Zohar sides with quantum theory. Both favor the observer, man, with a vital role in the nature of cosmic reality. Both present human consciousness as having the unique ability to influence and even radically alter the physical nature of the universe.

An incredible case of human dominion over celestial bodies is found in the Bible, concerning the cosmic miracles of the successor of Moses, Joshua Ben Nun. While pursuing the Amorites at Beth-Horon, Joshua Ben Nun directed the sun and the moon to stand still, we are told, for the course of a whole day, thus assuring an Israelite victory.

Scriptures declare: "...for the Lord harkened unto the voice of man."[1] According to the *Book of Joshua*, the Earth's rotation about the Sun was interrupted by the command of Joshua, who implored this cosmic disruption before the eyes of Israel. That celestial bodies, whose intrinsic intelligence dictates movement along precise, predestined orbital paths, obeyed the command of Joshua is indicated in the following passage:

"And he said in the sight of Israel, 'Sun stand still upon Gibeon, and the moon, stay in the valley of Ajalon.' And the sun stood still, and the moon stayed until the people had avenged themselves upon their enemies."[2] A fantastic story indeed, and yet one that conforms with the quantum theory of the new age of physics.

Unlike Newtonian physics which excludes man's participation in the cosmic processes, quantum physics undermines Newtonian determinism, inasmuch as the observer becomes a participant in what he is observing and actually determines the outcome of the experiment according to what he chooses to see. Having arrived at the conclusion that thought can change the physical world, it is a small conceptual step to the kabbalistic idea that celestial energy can be directed by the thoughts of man.

With this in mind, let us return to our narration of Rabbi Akiva's daughter as related in the previous chapter. The capacity to change our destiny through our deeds and actions does not necessarily contradict the idea of a mechanistic universe. The alternative to living in a mechanistic frame of reference is to reach another, higher dimension. Rabbi Akiva's daughter elevated her consciousness to a place where the predictability of the mechanistic laws no longer applied.[3] The Zohar provides many examples of altering the predictable.

Rabbi Abba was one day sitting at the gate of Lydda when he saw a weary traveler seat himself on a ledge and there he fell asleep. Rabbi Abba saw a serpent glide up towards the man, but before it reached him, a huge bird swept down and ate the snake. The sleeping man awoke, saw the dead snake in front of him, moved away, and no sooner had he done so when the ledge gave way, and fell into a hollow below leaving the man unharmed.

Rabbi Abba approached him, saying: "Tell me, what have you done that the Lord should perform two miracles for you?" The man replied: "Never did anyone do an injury to me, but that I made peace with him and forgave him. Moreover, if I could not make peace with him, I did not retire to rest before I forgave him, together with all those who vexed me. Nor was I at any time concerned about the evil that any man did me; I exerted myself to show kindness to such a man."

Hearing this, Rabbi Abba wept and said: "This man's deeds excel even those of Joseph.[4] For Joseph showed compassion towards his own brethren, but this man did more, and it was thus befitting that the Lord perform for him one miracle upon another."[5]

We are provided with a further demonstration of the link between astral influences and the predictable in the following parable, freely translated from the Zohar:

Rabbi Hiyah and Rabbi Jose were approaching a mountain when they saw two men going along. A beggar approached one of the two and said, "I beg of you, give me some food, even if only a piece of bread because for two days I have been wandering in the wilderness without any food."

One of the two men thereupon took out the food and drink which he had brought with him for the journey and gave it to the poor man. Ravenous, the poor man ate all the food the man had except for a single crust of bread. This too was given to the poor man for the road.

His companion asked him, "What will you do for food? For I am going to eat my own and I shall not share with you." The other replied, "Do I depend on or want to eat yours?"

The two men resumed their journey. Rabbi Hiyah and Rabbi Jose followed. Soon, the man who had given all his food away became faint with hunger. Said his companion to him, "did I not tell you not to share your bread with the poor man?" Overhearing this, Rabbi Hiyah whispered to Rabbi Jose, "We have sufficient food, let us give him some bread." Rabbi Jose responded, "Would you snatch from him the merit of his good deed? Let us follow and watch the outcome, for assuredly the pallor of death is on this man's face. I believe the Lord has prepared the entire incident for him in order to deliver him."

They followed and shortly the man who was faint with hunger feil asleep under a tree and his companion left him. Rabbi Jose then said to Rabbi Hiyah, "Now we shall observe a miracle." And indeed, it was not long before a fiery adder came to rest by the man's side.

Said Rabbi Hiyah, "Woe unto this man, for he shall surely die now." Rabbi Jose replied, "No. He deserves that a miracle should be done on his behalf." And lo, another snake slithered down from the tree with the intent to kill the man, but the fiery adder attacked and killed it before turning its head and departing.

Rabbi Jose said, "Did I not tell you that the Lord would perform a miracle for him, and that you should not deprive him of his merit by offering him food?"

Soon afterward, the man awoke and stood to leave. Rabbi Hiyah and Rabbi Jose approached him and gave him food. When he had eaten, Rabbi Hiyah informed him of the miracle which the Lord had performed for him.

Hence it is written, "Righteousness delivers from death,"[6] Why? Because righteousness is the Tree of Life, and it rouses itself against the Tree of Death.[7]

Rabbi Jose rightly believed that the astral influence which might have impelled the demise of this individual would be overcome by his supreme act of sharing. And

so it was. The astrological pattern was changed by the
deeds of a man, thus proving the kabbalistic axiom, "the
stars impel, they do not compel."

The significance that seems to emerge from the Zohar is the
need to establish within ourselves the kabbalistic understanding
of cause and effect. The Zohar recognized the futility of the
rationale which links cause irrevocably with effect. A man's
actions, even though they may be separated from their effects
by time, space and motion, are not lost and forgotten. The
altruistic acts of the characters in the Zoharic narrations
demonstrated their empathy, sensitivity, and understanding.
Their positive consciousness and kind deeds, while long since
gone in the physical realm, nevertheless maintained a
continuity.

Thus, whatever fate might have been in store for these
individuals was transformed. The celestial energies, established
for the purpose of correcting a previous incarnation, impelled
the Force in a manner that coincided with the soul's tikune or
corrective process. Positive action, a necessary ingredient in
revising the cycle of correction, was activated by the
participants in both narrations. The link with positive activity
took place before the stars were able to execute their
predetermined result. Their sincere concern for their fellow man
upset the karmic blueprint put in force by the stars.

The preceding Zohar points to a reconciliation of the
seeming randomness of quantum mechanics, the determinism of
Newtonian physics, and the free will of man. Cosmic
determinism dictated the condition by which the participants
would meet their deaths. However, in each case the
protagonist's preference for positive consciousness transformed

a predetermined selection of death to a free will decision to live.

According to Newtonian theory, the universe acts not unlike a giant clock, unwinding towards a predictable and unalterable final state. From the Newtonian perspective, human beings are little more than cogs in the wheels of some colossal cosmic mechanism. Quantum physics offers humankind the capability to influence the physical universe, but little in the way of free will. Kabbalah teaches that consciousness can integrate all disparities, mental, physical, and spiritual.

There are two parallel universes,[8] one, the flawless Tree of Life reality, where past, present and future exist as undifferentiated aspects of the divine continuum, and where negative human activity is immediately reconciled. The other, the illusionary Tree of Knowledge reality exists solely for the purpose of allowing man free will sufficient to alleviate Bread of Shame. It is this illusionary reality which contains the fragmentation of time, chaos and disorder. The Tree of Knowledge reality is the domain of those who abandon themselves to the Desire to Receive for the Self Alone. The Tree of Life reality is reserved for those who exercise restriction over the negative aspect of desire and thus manifest Desire to Receive for the Sake of Sharing.

From the kabbalistic perspective, free will consists of one decision. Either one selects a course of positive consciousness and becomes linked with the total contentment provided by the Tree of Life reality, or one chooses the the illusionary Tree of Knowledge realm of chaos and disorder, only to raise the question "why me?" when misfortune suddenly takes control over their lives.

Consequently, the kabbalist steers clear of the realm of physical illusion and makes every attempt to connect with the all-seeing, all-knowing reality of the Tree of Life and thus bring his life and environment into perfect harmony with the cosmos.[9]

Who in his right mind would hurt his fellow man if he knew the act would cause his own heart attack? Who would risk the danger of cancer produced as a direct result of an imbalance in his Desire to Receive? Who, if he could see the deadly effects of his negative actions, would be so stupid as to engage in such actions?

The illusion that we live in a chaotic universe where events occur accidentally is one of the many common misconceptions Kabbalah attempts to destroy. In fact, all the misfortunes that befall us are the direct result of our own negative behavior and past life decisions, regardless of how distant in time the cause may be from the effect. By restricting the negative aspect of desire, we activate the Tree of Life consciousness, in essence releasing ourselves from the doctrine of reincarnation which dictates that if one involves himself in negative activity in one lifetime, one must suffer a replay of his past mistakes in the next.

The Kabbalah is clear in its insistence that an indeterminate universe is necessary to establish free will. For the negative individual, free will is an illusion.

Have you noticed that the conclusion that we do not have the power to influence events often arises when misfortune befalls us? Though most of us would admit that we do exert some influence on the outcome of mundane events, we have strong misgivings concerning our ability to make lasting changes in our lives. In fact, bad things happen only to those who are trapped in the illusionary reality. If we choose to move up to a higher, more positive, altered state of consciousness, we arrive at a flawless universe with a perfect structure of order, happiness and fulfillment.

Had more people been exposed to kabbalistic concepts and the reasons behind them, less emphasis would certainly be placed on material values. In no way is this a negation of physical reality, which is of vital importance to the soul's cycle of correction. However, we should always remember and temper our physical actions with a knowledge that it is the metaphysical reality from which we came and to which we must return.

This idea is supported by Quantum Physics which contends that matter, when viewed from the subatomic perspective, is totally devoid of material substance. According to quantum theory, the so-called physical world has no material basis. Subatomic "particles," the "building blocks" of nature, the underlying "structure" of the physical world, are in fact something which might best be described as metaphysical "tendencies to become."

There is a strong possibility that the metaphysical realm may never be scientifically verified. This is of no concern to the kabbalist. For even if no observer ever validates empirically the existence of the flawless, metaphysical realm, neither will science refute its presence. Indeed, with the uncertainty principle, science can no longer claim dominion over the material realm or even prove its existence.

If you find it hard to question the presence of the physical reality, you are by no means alone. We have all been programmed since childhood to believe that what we can feel, taste, touch and see is all there is. It is not surprising, then, that we have difficulty coming to grips with the idea that the physical world is an illusion. The idea that matter at its essence is immaterial leaves us with a feeling that there isn't much that we can safely lean upon. Yet stubborn insistence on outdated values and perspectives will do nothing to improve our physical, mental, emotional, or spiritual well being.

Since the time of the Patriarch Abraham, the Hebrews demonstrated an uncanny perception of rudimentary physics. Though not in the modern language of mathematics, the early kabbalists made practical application of their grasp of the Force and astral influences. To them, the Hebrew letters, the names of twenty-two distinct and astonishingly powerful energy-intelligences, are animated with a spiritual force that is more immense than atomic energy. But the Aleph Beth is of no practical use if we do not understand how to patch ourselves into this supreme, all-encompassing network. Kabbalah is a program that allows us access to this life-affirming system known as the Tree of Life.

The answers to life's most intractable mysteries are bound up within the way we think and how we act. In his *Gate of Elevated Consciousness*, the Ari describes what must occur when consciousness affects matter.

When a person does a good deed, he makes manifest and acquires a personal positive intelligent life force. All essence within our universe has been structured by the actions of man. For even the sound that emanates from striking a stone with a rod is not in vain. It maintains its rightful place in the cosmos. Even from man's word of mouth are created angelic metaphysical life forces. These very same forces become chariots integrated with the whole of the cosmos. They then connect with the souls of the righteous of the past. Through this interconnectedness, these life form energy-intelligences then serve as providers of cosmic intelligences. They assist the creator (man) of these forces, who become chariots for cosmic intelligence.[10]

The Israelites were furnished with a system by which they could transcend the illusionary realm. By virtue of displaying positive energy-consciousness, the Hebrew Aleph Beth could serve positive individuals in supporting their activity to achieve communion with the Tree of Life universe. Consequently, the statement, "There are no astral influences on the nation of Israel" did apply to those who could tap the awesome power of the Cosmos through their knowledge and practical use of the Aleph Beth. Those Israelites and others ignorant of the knowledge of celestial bodies and unaware of the immense power of the Aleph Beth would, however, remain in the universe of illusion and misfortune.

Thus, we have before us the system by which one can achieve a cosmic connection with the Tree of Life, the Hebrew Aleph Beth. We have also come to the answer of the question raised earlier as to whether or not there is *Mazal* (astral influence) for the nation of Israel.

Again, I will risk the annoyance of many astrologers by quoting the Zohar: "And the wisdom of their words was lost."[11] The Zohar's statement that the wisdom of their words "was lost" refers to the wisdom of the ancient Egyptians, whose understanding of the internal had forever been concealed. Like many astrologers today, the Egyptians had spiritual power but did not know how to use it. As the Zohar goes on to explain, "the Egyptians had no knowledge of the initial creation of celestial bodies. Their knowledge was based only on the external movements of the planets that are observed in their celestial orbits."[12] Kabbalistic astrology, contrarily, seeks to understand the internal structure of creation, the realm of the Force.

The Zohar's explanation of the foregoing verse reveals the general pattern of duality upon which all creation is structured: the physical and metaphysical, the external and the internal. Man, in whom we find both a body and a soul, is no differently constructed.

With the help of the kabbalistic blueprint of our universe, we will be amazed at the extent to which we can control our environments and, more importantly, our own futures. To alter or transform a predetermined course requires both foresight and a willingness to change our behavior. The signs of the Zodiac will be our guideposts, our shields and our weapons, in the struggle against the forces of chaos.

With knowledge of Kabbalah, the spiritual astrologer can predict with uncanny accuracy specific dates on which particular events are going to take place. An astrologer may also reveal aspects about the character of an individual that, had they been known earlier, could have averted many a family or personal crisis. If a prediction spells doom or misfortune, however, the astrologer must be careful to assure the individual that with the proper attitude of restriction he or she can deflect disaster.

The history of the Jewish people, perhaps to a greater degree than that of any other nation, has been marked by the conflict between the spiritual and the physical realities. This is still very much of a problem. Few today would deny the necessity of an infusion in the world of spiritual energy. The dwindling ranks of all religions only serves to underscore the need for a renewal of the esoteric tradition of the Kabbalah. The key to the coming of the Messiah and a finale to human carnage can be found in the knowledge and practice of this ancient art.

We are indeed fortunate to be living in the Messianic Age of Aquarius.[13] For the tools and mechanisms for change which were hidden for so long are again available. The metaphysical connection with which the Hebrews dealt the first time, is again accessible to all who have the will and the knowledge to use it. It is the energy of the Great Exodus on stage for yet another encore.

From the Zohar we learn why and just how deeply the secrets of the Kabbalah were hidden:

It is said that, one day Rabbi Jose entered a cavern and at the far end found a book hidden in the cleft of a rock. He brought it out and caught sight of seventy-two tracings of letters which had been given to Adam. He (Adam) knew all the wisdom of the supernal beings and all those beings that abide behind the klippot which manifest behind the veil protecting the celestial essences. He knew all that was destined to happen in the world.[14]

He called Rabbi Judah and the two began to examine
the book. After reading only two or three of the letters
they caught glimpses of the supernal wisdom. But as
soon as they began to delve more deeply, a fiery flame
struck their hands and the book vanished from them.

They went to Rabbi Shimon and told him what had
occurred. Rabbi Shimon asked them, "Were you perhaps
scrutinizing those letters which dealt with the coming of
the Messiah?" Rabbis Jose and Judah could not answer,
for they had forgotten everything. Rabbi Shimon told
them, "The Lord does not desire that so much should be
revealed to the world, but when the days of the Messiah
will be at hand, even the little children will discover the
secrets of wisdom. At that time it will be revealed to all,
as it is written: 'For then I will turn to the peoples a
pure language.'"[15]

Thus will the new spirit find its expression in the ideal of
Kabbalah and open new spheres of consciousness during the
Messianic era.

*Why*

*are there righteous men*
*who are physical wrecks*
*while many unrighteous men*
*are hale and hearty?*

DO YOU EVER GET THE FEELING THAT SOMEONE OR SOMETHING
out there doesn't like you?

Early kabbalists were intimately familiar with the celestial
bodies and regarded their movements across the heavens as
physical expressions of extraterrestrial intelligence. They viewed
the constellations and planets as intelligent entities, motivated
by internal energies which manifest on Earth as the four
elements — water, fire, air and earth.

As strange as this idea seems today, the early kabbalists'
observations of the universe, inspired by the reflections on the
Zohar, enabled them to provide a valid guide for the individual
searching for the improvement of his physical, emotional and
mental well-being. More importantly, they provided a discipline
which could take the aspirant to a higher level of awareness and
moral conduct.

The Sun and Moon exert the most direct influence over Earth's inhabitants; the astral influences of the planetary bodies, Saturn, Jupiter, Mars, Venus and Mercury also affect us, but to a lesser degree. Through astrology, we become aware of how these cosmic intelligences operate and learn how to make use of them.

In astrology, there is a recognition of the weak and strong forces that move the universe and motivate the individual. Knowledge of these characteristics helps us to discover causes and relationships between our own actions and those of the cosmos. The internal knowledge of astrology, concealed in Abraham's *Book of Formation*, stressed that whenever an individual gains a conceptual understanding of one of these characteristics he or she activates that part of the force within themselves. Such connections are most often experienced internally, taking the form of "brainstorms" or moments of inspiration or extreme lucidity. Occasionally, they manifest physically, in "visitations" or other such phenomena.

The Zohar[1] tells us that the positive energy of the Sun exerts less influence upon the Moon when the Moon is in its descending phase than when it is in its ascending phase. The author attributes this to the negative, or "left column" influence which becomes increasingly dominant beginning on the fifteenth day of the Moon's cycle and lasts until the final day. This intriguing description concerning the interaction between the moon and the sun is the basis of an astonishing Zoharic conclusion.[2] As the Moon's cycle represents a gradual revealment and concealment of positive and negative energy (good and evil), and because the Moon reflects the destinies of man, one should avoid venturing into any new undertaking from the 16th day of the lunar month to the day preceding the coming of the succeeding month.

Why, asks the Zohar, are there righteous men who are physical wrecks while many unrighteous men are hale and hearty? One might speculate that the latter were born of virtuous parents while the former, although righteous themselves, were not children of righteous parents. The facts, however, reason against this, since we see many honest and honorable men who are the sons of worthy parents who nevertheless suffer a variety of physical and spiritual ills.[3]

Let us examine the position of fate and determinism as it is understood by the Kabbalah.

The Zohar and other mystical doctrines of the ancients shed light on this subject. In essence, they tell us that there is a period when the Moon is "defective," a time when "judgment" is visited upon her and the Sun is hidden from her. It is the Moon that, in all times and seasons, releases souls to enter the sons of men, having previously gathered them for that purpose. A soul released during the period when the Moon is on the wane — more specifically, when she begins to descend after the 15th day of the lunar month — will be the potential victim of degradation, poverty and chastisement, whether or not he or she is sinful or righteous; while the souls which the Moon sends forth when the Moon is in the grade of ascension are likely to enjoy an abundance of riches, children and health, all on account of the Mazal that flows forth and joins itself to that grade in order to be perfected and blessed by it.

We therefore see that much is dependent upon Mazal (astral influence) and that a person's length of life, children, and livelihood are not totally dependent on one's merits. Rather much depends on the particular astral influence at birth, Mazal.

Does this mean that the Zohar condemns us to lives of misery or good fortune without giving us the opportunity to intervene or share in our destiny? No. As I previously mentioned, the dictum of "there is no Mazal to the nation of Israel" refers to those who are ignorant and have not had the opportunity to rise above the determination of Mazal. Consequently, it is wise for each of us to seek an altered state of consciousness which will allow us to rise above our a predetermined frame of misfortune.

What emerges from the foregoing Zohar is that the planets and constellations present constant forces in the universe. For conceptual purposes, these forces of the constellations can be pictured as the carriers of the energy-intelligence. Modulated by the interaction of planetary influences, these forces are exerted on the renewal and birth of souls.

Previous to this time, the concepts presented here were the preserve of a handful of sages, mystics, prophets and holy people who, by reaching elevated levels of consciousness, have seen the world in all its majestic beauty. Fortunately, the Age of Aquarius will be a period of universal enlightenment, in which the secrets of the Kabbalah will be available to one and all.

As the Prophet Jeremiah predicted concerning this epoch-making period, "and they shall teach no more every man his neighbor, and every man his brother, saying, know the Lord.

Rather everyone shall know Me, from the smallest to the oldest."[4]

# Part Three

## Cosmic Danger Zones

# 13 Monthly Danger Zones

And the Lord said unto Abram:
Go out from your land and from
your birthplace and from the
house of your father.[1]

# How

does the choice of
day affect the planned
activity?

THE ABOVE COMMANDMENT TOLD ABRAHAM TO LEAVE THE house of the Moon, the house of Saturn, and the house of Mars. For when the houses of Mars, Saturn and Moon prevail, one should not venture into a new undertaking.

According to the biblical code, the negative energy-intelligence known as Purgatory emerged on the second day of creation. As the energy which brought Purgatory into being was of a negative quality, kabbalists denote the second day of the week, Monday, as a day of intensified negative activity. Described by the ancient texts as an embodiment of this negative energy, Mars, the "Red Planet," is associated with the second day and is thus considered a negative influence.

On the fourth day of creation, the moon is said to have undergone a negative transformation from her original sun-filled condition.[2] Thus the fourth day, Wednesday, is linked with brilliance. On the fourth day, this "poverty stricken" condition of diminished lunar activity prevails over all earthly activity. Evil individuals fall into her clutches on this day, while the righteous seek refuge from her.[3]

To undertake a new venture at the wrong time is like planting a seed in an inappropriate season. It simply will not grow. When started at an inopportune time, the likelihood of inviting misfortune, whether it be a mismatch in marriage or business is much greater. Therefore, one should be very wary about entering into any new venture or agreement on a Monday or a Wednesday, the second and fourth days of the week.[4]

The less we expose ourselves to environmental and celestial negativity the better. Keeping clear of negative celestial invasion results in a conservation of energy. Hence, the need to resupply our weakened immune systems and to energize our devitalized fountains of energy becomes less of a daily chore. In fact, if the activity of most of Earth's inhabitants were positive, there would be no danger zones. It is only because Earth's inhabitants continue in a negative direction that the danger zones manifest and prevent negative individuals from avoiding the violence and disruptions so prevalent in the material world.

Let us examine some other danger zones that should be avoided if we are to assure ourselves lives of health and well-being.

"And the woman conceived and bore a son; and when she saw him that he was a goodly child, she hid him three months."[5] The three months mentioned here allude to a secret implication. The Zohar informs us that the lunar months of

Tammuz, Av and Tevet manifest an unusual degree of cosmic negative activity and influence.[6] Concealment of the infant offered protection from the harsh, severe judgment that reigns in the universe during these months. It is no coincidence that these three Hebrew months are linked to the destruction of the Holy Temple.

Tevet, the name of the tenth month of the Jewish lunar year, with the zodiac sign of Capricorn, is ruled by the planet Saturn. The 10th day of Tevet commemorates the beginning of the siege of Jerusalem by Nebuchadnezzar.[7] This day has been proclaimed as a fast day according to Talmudic Law.[8]

Tammuz is the name of the fourth month of the Jewish year. Its zodiac sign is Cancer. The 17th day of Tammuz commemorates five calamities which befell the nation of Israel. A communal fast was decreed by the sages of the Talmud as the day of the breaching of the walls of Jerusalem by Nebuchadnezzar (586 B.C.E.) and Titus (70 C.E.).

Four other calamities occurred on the 17th day of Tammuz: the tablets of the Law were broken by Moses;[9] the daily offering ceased in the First Temple; Apostomos burned the Torah in the Sanctuary and erected an idol there.[10]

Av is the name of the fifth month in the Jewish year. The zodiac sign of this month is Leo. The traditional days in the month of Av begin with the anniversary of the death of the High Priest Aaron on the first day of Av.[11] The ninth of Av commemorates the destruction of the First and Second Temple. The First Temple, ƀuilt by King Solomon, was destroyed by the Babylonian king, Nebuchadnezzar in 586 B.C.E., on the 9th of Av.  The Second Temple was destroyed by the Romans in 70

C.E. on the 9th of Av. The Talmud[12] also states that on the 9th
of Av it was decreed, that the Children of Israel, after the
exodus from Egypt, should not enter Israel. The expulsion of
the Jews from Spain in 1492 is said also to have occurred on
the 9th of Av.

The misfortune which takes place during these three months
is the result of negative cosmic forces. The hazards and pitfalls
that many of us encounter can be traced to our having come
under the influence of these periods of negative energy. Hence
it is wise to be cognizant of the danger zones and careful to
avoid them.

It is wrong to think that Jerusalem is considered the Holy
City simply because the Holy Temple was located there.
Jerusalem is the Holy City because it is an immensely powerful
energy center, and therefore, as a natural consequence, the Holy
Temple was built there. Yet, one cannot avoid the obvious
connection between Jerusalem and the kind of overheating and
explosive reactions which are an all too familiar fixture in
Jerusalem and the surrounding area.

Certain times and places speak strongly of an underlying
force responsible for a world of order and beauty. Yet we
cannot close our eyes to the pain, violence and chaos that make
their presence so cruelly felt. The problem rests with *Dinim*
(ungovernable energy).

During the months of Tammuz, Av and Tevet, the energy of
the Force is such that there is no revelation of the Shekhinah
(the appropriate cosmic vessel which insures the manifestation
and stability of the Force). At such times the dynamic intensity
of the Force is so severe that no vessel is capable of making

contact with, or handling the energy of the Force, which thereby manifests as Dinim in the universe.[13]

The Force might aptly be compared to the energy which enters our homes through the electric wires. Controlled it is of immense value, uncontrolled it can be destructive and downright dangerous. Switch on a light, for example, and you receive a wonderful blessing, but stick your finger in a socket and the same energy provides you with a horrible curse.

The Temple was structured in such a way as to provide a channel for the supreme energy of the Force and give nourishment, peace and prosperity to all inhabitants of Earth. The Ark of the Covenant was the instrument by which the Force was drawn.

The Israelites understood that celestial forces are governed by the activity of man. Thus, instead of being pawns in the cosmic scheme, as other ancients had believed, the Israelites understood man to be the prime interface between the terrestrial and the celestial forces of the metaphysical domain. Only when the forces are in balance do the heavens declare their majesty and influence.

During Tammuz, Av and Tevet, in the absence of the Temple, the violence that threatens our planet cannot be halted. Within the framework of Tammuz, Av and Tevet there is very little that the average person can do to influence the cosmic forces. As mentioned, however, certain individuals of extraordinary spiritual ability can channel these forces. Kabbalists have specific meditations designed to reduce the intensity of the Force during such times and thus make It beneficial. Having accomplished these meditations, the

Shekhinah transforms the immense power of the Force, thus permitting the kabbalist to function even in an environment of violence and chaos.

The Force must undergo a reduction in order to operate as a viable circuit of energy here on earth. Variations in the revealed energy of the Force influence the beginning of new ventures, inasmuch as the lifeblood of a new venture and its potential success depends on the ability of the Force to make itself manifest. During Tammuz, Av and Tevet, the Force is in a state of *Katnut*, a decreased level of activity, hence the increased chance that a new venture will have a negative outcome.

We move now to another cosmic event, which manifested some 3,200 years ago at the time of the Exodus and not, as might have been expected, at the "Beginning," some 5,700 years ago. Egyptian mastery of the power of evil influence rendered the people of Israel incapable, on their own, of overcoming the negative energy-intelligence that held them and the entire world in bondage.

The difference in spiritual structure between the Egyptians and the other peoples of Earth before the Exodus was so slight as to render any distinction between them undefinable. Only through the intervention of the Force was the Exodus of humankind from spiritual bondage possible. It was only an enormous concentration and intensified infusion of the positive energy emanating from the Force that enabled the Hebrews to overcome the power of their slave masters.[14]

The dual nature of the creative process encompasses the two polarities of desire, Desire to Receive for the Sake of Sharing and the Desire to Receive for the Self Alone.[15] Without the possibility of choosing between these two aspects there could be no free will. The Desire to Receive for the Self Alone, which embodied the consciousness of the Egyptian masters, is necessary within the creative process. If the opportunity to do evil were not present, the individual's ability to choose the path of righteousness, indeed, the whole purpose of creation, would be thwarted. Thus the removal of Bread of Shame[16] would remain eternally unresolved and the *Tsimtsum*, the original restriction,[17] would have been in vain.

The events that occurred on and before the night of the 15th day of Nissan represented a temporary phenomenon, accomplished for the purpose of releasing the energies of freedom and exodus. Freedom! Exodus! These were achieved not by humankind's efforts, but rather through the grace of the Lord. On the day after, the 16th day of Nissan, the entire energy-intelligence of the Force reverted to its former state as unrevealed energy, thereby recreating the cosmic void.

Thus the period from the 16th day of Nissan to the 6th day of the month of Sivan remained in a state of diminished energy, wherein the cosmos became dominated by a negative state of consciousness. In Hebrew this is called by the code name *Katnut*.[18]

Through the meditation method of *Sfirat Omer* the *sfirot* are employed to gradually restore the Force to a manifested state. While the kabbalist provides us with the necessary support equipment to lessen the effects of the decreased cosmic energy-intelligence, nonetheless, these periods of reduced energies will have a deleterious effect on new undertakings.

This period commences from the 16th day of the lunar month Nissan and continues until the 6th day of the lunar month of Sivan. These dates will vary in the Gregorian calendar from March 24th to June 4th. One should be in possession of a lunar calendar and observe from the 16th day of lunar Aries to the 5th day of lunar Gemini as dates to avoid when contemplating new ventures.

It should be known that the Hebrew month of Sivan is governed by the astral sign of Gemini.

The roots of most misfortunes can be traced to the cosmic danger zones. Armed with the knowledge of these zones, we can transcend the realm of chance, luck, and indetermination, and bring order, fulfillment, and supreme tranquility to our lives.

*Why*

*is Scorpio considered the "bitter" sign of the Zodiac?*

OUR FINAL COSMIC DANGER ZONE IS THE LUNAR MONTH OF Scorpio, or its Hebrew equivalent, Heshvan, the eighth month of the lunar year. The name occurs in the *Book of Formation*[1] and later branches of rabbinic literature, but nowhere in the Bible itself. Strangely enough, the Patriarch Abraham, in the *Book of Formation*, added the prefix "Mar" to the word Heshvan, which means "bitter," making it *Marheshvan*.

Many theories have been suggested as to why Heshvan should have been so described. It is somewhat of a mystery, too, that while Marheshvan is a trademark of misfortune, chaos and disorder, this month was not included along with the three negative months mentioned previously by the Zohar.

In its earliest occurrence, Marheshvan extends from October 6th to November 4th, and its latest, from November 4th to

December 3rd. Some historical days recorded in Marheshvan were the blinding of King Zedekiah by the command of Nebuchadnezzer[2] and the death on the 11th of Rachel, the wife of Jacob, the Patriarch.[3] Marheshvan has the distinction of being the only month in which no cosmic energy event (holy day) takes place.

Amongst the historic days in Marheshvan, the 17th day stands out significantly above all the others. For this is the day of the commencement, in Noah's time, of the flood which brought about the annihilation of all humankind, along with the animal and vegetable kingdoms.[4]

Following the kabbalistic principle[5] that physically manifested events are the results of cosmic influence, these events, just listed, however significant, cannot be considered the cause of Abraham's decision to add the prefix "mar" (bitter) to the month of Heshvan. Let us therefore explore the cosmic determinant that brought Scorpio to be considered the bitter sign of the Zodiac.

A good starting point in our investigation is the Book of Genesis where we find that of the twelve tribes of Israel, Scorpio is represented by Dan[6] the son of Jacob by Bilah.[7] When Dan was born, Rachel cried out, "The Lord hath judged me, and hath also heard my voice, and hath given me a son." Therefore she named him Dan.

Those readers somewhat familiar with the biblical text under consideration might question the selection of Dan as the celestial dominion of the zodiac sign of Scorpio. A study of the text should place the tribe of Gad as the channel-influence over Scorpio, the reason being that Gad was the eighth son of the twelve born to Jacob, and Scorpio is the eighth sign of the zodiac which begins with the sign of Aries. Indeed, the family tree of Jacob has prompted many astrologers to associate Gad with Scorpio in their determination of the positive and negative traits of Scorpio.

And yet, the Rabad[8] chooses Dan to characterize the traits of Scorpio. Here is yet another indication that the Bible is not merely the root of a religion, but rather a cosmic code. The Rabad guards always against literal interpretations of ancient esoteric texts, and is especially watchful when interpreting biblical writings.

In the view of the Zohar, the tales and parables of the Torah are symbolic reflections of the inner metaphysical realm through which one could perceive the divine mysteries of the universe. Rabbi Shimon Bar Yohai berates those who take these simple tales as relating only to incidents in the lives of individuals or nations. They pertain to the inner lives of every person on earth.

This is not to suggest that a literal interpretation of the Bible does not make good reading, it does. And, indeed, it cannot be denied that the Bible provides a most valuable historical record. The reason the kabbalist probes beneath the surface of biblical interpretation is the result of an unshakable conviction that the real meaning of the Bible, like the Light Itself, must remain concealed. Only a fool judges a man by his clothes; so too is he who considers only the outer garments of the Bible.[9]

Consequently, for the kabbalist, the superficial relationship between the tribe of Gad as the eighth son and Scorpio as the eighth sign of the zodiac does not reveal the essence of the astrological meaning concerning Scorpio. For the Rabad, blessed with the knowledge of Kabbalah, Scorpio is understood to be linked with the tribe of Dan.

Let us, therefore, return to our investigation of Marheshvan, Scorpio, and, more importantly, the deeper metaphysical implications of Dan, of whom Scorpio is considered the mirror image. When Dan was born, Rachel cried out, "and the Lord hath judged me." This is an allusion to the enormous power inherent in this sign as well as to the principle of judgment.[10]

"Those that pitch their tent on the east side of the Ark was the tribe of Judah..."[11] "...And on the north side shall be the flag of Dan."[12]

These verses, if read superficially, are incomprehensible to the student of the Bible. However, this entire section of Numbers contains for the kabbalist the very essence of true astrology and the information necessary for the attainment of spiritual awareness and the improvement of health and well-being.

The question raised by the Zohar is why is the flag of the tribe of Dan positioned on the north side of the energy-tracking station of the Ark? What for that matter was the significance and implication of the journey of the Ark itself?

The coded word "journey" indicates the presence of a manifested state of the Force. Scripture states, "...and the Ark of the Covenant of the Lord went before them three days' journey, to seek a resting place for them."[13] Here, a resting place means the unification between *Ze'ir Anpin* (the Force) and *Malkhut* (the recipient). However, to prepare *Malkhut* for unification (circuitry), the Ark travelled "three days," this being a coded message that referred to the establishment of the three column system.[14]

This was the Ark that was carried by the Levites during their wandering through the Sinai desert. When the Force became manifested by the three column system, the Ark contained cosmic energy vital to Israel's conquest of the Holy Land.[15]

The first to begin the journey was the flag of Judah[16] from the east, guided by the sfirotic force of the central column, *Tifereth*, corresponding to the extraterrestrial camp of Uriel; this was followed by the flag of the camp of Reuben,[17] corresponding to the extraterrestrial camp of Michael on the south side, under the influence of the right column sfirotic force of *Hesed*, symbolic of the coded significance of the south-east of the altar of the Tabernacle.[18]

The sprinkling of the blood on the altar began first at the southeast corner of the altar.

Then came the camp of Ephraim, on the west, guided by the sfirotic force of *Malkhut*, corresponding to the extraterrestrial camp of Raphael,[19] and finally, the flag of Dan, on the north, guided by the sfirotic force of the left column (judgment) corresponding to the extraterrestrial camp of Gabriel.[20]

The sprinkling of the blood on the altar was also at the northwest corner.

The whole was linked together and was unified in the Divine Name of the Tetragrammaton, which is both the starting-point and the consummation of the all-embracing reality, the Force.

Therefore, *Ephraim* (*Malkhut*) followed Reuben to unite with *Hesed*, and when *Malkhut* became manifest with the other two, right and central, she then combined and received the Force, the Light of Wisdom.[21]

What emerges from the preceding Zohar is the significance of Dan's awesome power as a channel for the Force. Therefore, Rachel cried out, "the Lord hath judged me, and also heard my voice," indicating the sfirotic force of *Gevurah* (Judgment), the channel of the Force which became manifest, indicated by Rachel's exclamation of the phrase "heard my voice."

The reader may now find even more puzzling the "bitter" definition that Abraham associated with the month of Heshvan. In fact, one might expect Heshvan to be considered a most powerful, energy-intelligent force, precisely for the reason that the extraterrestrial superforce of Gabriel is motivated and manifested by the presence of the immensely powerful Dan channel.

The Zohar, however, referring to the coded phrase "three days journey" makes the point that establishment of the Force hinges on the performance of the "three days," or the other three sfirotic energy-intelligences, namely, east, south and west. If this condition is not met, then we are vulnerable, during the dominion of the constellation of Scorpio, to havoc and chaos due to the Divine Name of the Tetragrammaton becoming manifested without the proper supportive dimensions of the vessel. This is awesome power running amuck, without the intervention of a controlled system of checks and balances.

Consequently, Heshvan is Mar, "bitter," but not necessarily destructive. The Hebrew word for *Mar* consists of two letters of the Hebrew alphabet, Mem and Resh.[22] However, when placing the Resh before the Mem, we come up with another word, *Ram*, which means "high" or "lofty". And therein lies the mystery of the fundamental essence of Scorpio, a sign of enormous power which can be positively or negatively used.

This idea has already been revealed by the Zoharic interpretation of another coded section of the Bible, the blessings of Jacob the Patriarch upon his twelve sons, the twelve signs of the zodiac.[23]

Dan shall judge his people, as one of the tribes of Israel. Dan shall be a serpent in the way, a horned snake in the path, that biteth the horse's heels, so that his rider falleth backward.

I wait for Thy Salvation, O Lord![24]

In the Zohar Rabbi Hiyah contended that the verse should have read, "Dan shall judge the tribes of Israel" or "Dan shall judge the tribes of Israel as one." What is the meaning of "Dan shall judge his people?" The explanation is as follows. Dan was the rear guard of the camps.[25] Therefore, Dan would judge his people, the tribes of Israel as one, that is, as the One, All-Embracing Whole Force. This was realized in Samson,[26] who single-handedly wrought judgment on the world, and both judged and put to death without the assistance of an advisor.

Thus Dan is sometimes compared to a serpent lying in wait. Dan is seen in this light because of the words, "That bites at the horse's heels," to protect all the other camps. Dan is the serpent that lies in wait at the end of the path and drives back those coming from the evil side.

Rabbi Elazar said that the serpent was one of the supports of the Throne, because on the throne of Solomon, there was a serpent attached to his scepter above the lions. Therefore Jacob prayed, saying, "I have waited for thy salvation, O Lord." Jacob mentioned the Lord's salvation of Dan because he saw here the might of the serpent setting in motion judgment.[27]

What seems to emerge from the Biblical text and its Zoharic interpretation is the concept of judgment and its position within the cosmos as the protector of the universe. With Dan chosen as the ultimate channel for the manifested state of the Force, the concept of "harsh judgment" was a natural consequence of its intrinsic character.

Gevurah represents judgment, not in a sense of punishment that we usually understand, but in the sense of the inevitable repercussions of giving vent to Desire to Receive without first removing the aspect of Bread of Shame. The Force has but one desire, and that is to share continuously of its endless beneficence. When Desire to Receive is aroused by any member of the human race, that desire is experienced by the Force, and its fulfillment is immediately forthcoming. Thus the idea of harsh judgment might be compared to an impulsive child sticking his finger in a socket. The resulting shock does not suggest any form of external punishment or judgment. Just as the force of electrical current requires an appropriate vessel, so too does the Force, in order to be properly contained and channelled, require a vessel adaptable to the conditions that must be met by removing Bread of Shame.[28]

The vessel, meaning ourselves, must be fully prepared and fine-tuned to handle the energy of the Force. This preparedness involves total inclusion of circuitry made possible by the establishment and manifestation of the three states of consciousness stated in the Zohar. Consequently, if mankind finds itself constantly in the midst of crises, the problem is not with the Force, but rather with the actions of man.

"Biting of the horse's heels" was a dire consequence for those ill-prepared to channel the beneficence of the Force, no less than our inability to accept the direct current of electricity.

Scorpio is a sign veiled in mystery. Like all forms of energy it remains in state of suspended animation, awaiting the opportune moment for revealment. Its presence is concealed until a vessel reveals the power source. Just as a minuscule atom when smashed releases concentrated energy which can be used for good or evil,[29] the energy of Dan and Scorpio, depending upon the human conductor, can be channeled towards positive purposes or become an instrument of destruction.

Scorpio is a sign very much governed by extremes, and it manifests this polarity with an intensity unmatched by any other sign. Therefore, one must be wary of starting any new venture during the lunar month of Heshvan, inasmuch as one must choose between the possibility of extreme polarities. The result of such an endeavor might manifest as *Mar*, bitter, or *Ram*, rising and transcending, either succeeding beyond our highest expectations or sinking into a quagmire of oblivion.

It is important that we acquire as deep an understanding of the central ideas of astrology as possible so as to strengthen our bond with the cosmos. Knowledge is the connection.[30] The importance of timing extends far beyond the purely physical aspect of existence. We read in Ecclesiastes, "There is a time for every purpose..."[31] The implication being that we must exert our freedom of choice to discover the time best suited to our purposes.

Any new beginning depends on proper timing. A child is considered as being born when it takes its first breath. At that precise moment, the entire cosmos, infused with an unerring universal rhythm, acts and provides us with an orchestrated channeling of a whole array of cosmic influences. At the instant of birth, all the prevailing energy-intelligences are introduced into the child through its first life's breath. This breath marks the beginning of the child's independent and particular destiny, outside the womb of its mother. The celestial conditions at that given moment in time set the tone for all that follows.

Not only must we know when the potentially harmful energy of the cosmos reigns, we must also be aware of times when the structure of the metaphysical universe is such that we can and should approach the positive energy intelligences of the cosmos and tap their awesome power.

Scorpio is a water sign, an embodiment of left column or negative energy. The internal character of water is one of positiveness, sharing and outpouring. Thus, each of the three water signs (Scorpio, Pisces and Cancer) function and express themselves within the framework of water and its intrinsic characteristic of positiveness.

Why then do kabbalists establish Scorpio as a negative water sign? This idea seems to run counter to the essential idea of water intelligence which expresses itself in a positive manner. Water seeks its own level. Why? Because water's energy-intelligence is one of sharing or extension. The negative aspect of water has to do with overexpansion, overextension, too much sharing. A surplus of water results in flooding. Too much sharing by a parent spoils a child. A business expanding too rapidly will likely end in failure. Hence Scorpio's negative designation.

The Light of Hasadim is a code contained within the kabbalistic lexicon. The Force, also referred to by its coded name, Light of Wisdom, must be enclosed and concealed within the Light of Hasadim (Mercy) for it to become revealed. The paradox of revealment or manifestation of the Force (energy) lies precisely in the ability of the vessel or Hasadim to conceal the energy.

Consider the plus and minus poles of a light bulb that jointly provide the revealment and manifestation of electricity. They are, in effect, two opposing forces that together provide a unified expression of the all-embracing whole, the Force. Why must there be a positive pole in the light bulb, when in fact it is the negative pole that draws the current? Because the positive pole provides the proper setting for the Force to become physically expressed. The positive pole, with its intrinsic Light of Hasadim, furnishes the energy which allows for expansion and extension.

The Light of Hasadim, the positive vessel, makes manifest the Force. While the negative pole draws the current towards the receptacle, it is nevertheless the positive pole, with its Light of Hasadim, that provides the glowing expression of the bulb when drawn through the central column or restriction of the filament. When all of humankind makes manifest the whole of cosmic Hasadim, on Succoth, the nine day harvest festival beginning on the eve of the 15th of Tishrei, the flow and manifestation of the Force to provide the life force for all of earth's inhabitants is tantamount to a dam suddenly having its floodgates opened. The onrushing waters could, if not properly channelled, bring flooding and havoc.

Consequently, the Zodiac sign of Scorpio puts us in a predicament. Hasadim, portrayed by water, extends life force to all of Earth's inhabitants. Yet, the cosmic force of Hasadim's sudden release of energy is also responsible for a great deal of negative behavior.

Thus, only those whose capacity for restriction is great are advised to contemplate new ventures in the month of Scorpio. For those few spiritually powerful souls, beginning a new venture during the eighth month, Heshvan, is appropriate and indeed advantageous. However, those lacking a great capacity for restriction, meaning those who are motivated solely by Desire to Receive for the Self Alone, will be unable to control Hasadim's energy and thus are advised not to begin new ventures at this time.

# Part Four

## The Friendly Cosmos

*is man's role and responsability
in the universal scheme?*

IN AN EVER DARK AND FRIGID UNIVERSE, OUR DESCENDANTS, scientists tell us, will no longer enjoy the light of the Sun. Our world will be sent whirling into the icy reaches of space. The oceans will freeze solid and the air we breathe will condense like hard frost. The human race will die along with all other life on Earth.

This haunting vision of the future is enough to frighten anyone, but let me reassure the reader, these scientists are not referring to life in the immediate future. In fact, they predict these dire circumstances somewhere in the vicinity of a trillion years from now.

I guess we can now breathe a little easier knowing that we have been given a new lease on life. At least we and our children will not have to face so bleak and dismal a tomorrow.

The most distressing aspect of the modern world is the gravity of its problems. I am inclined to believe that we shall remain on the brink of catastrophe. Even government leaders, politicians, scientists and others on whom we have become so dependent as our problem solvers have raised their hands in despair that we shall be able to cope with our present problems and those of the future.

While history shows that other civilizations have experienced dark days and have managed to recover, I believe that most aspects of the world's present problems make them qualitatively different from those of the past. Harmful agents have spread over most of the face of the globe. Acid rain has devastated our forests.

Advanced technological innovations have brought such unexpected problems as removal of nuclear waste, widespread use of pesticides to increase the world's food supply, and pollution of our streams and rivers. Dangerous levels of contamination to our fish, water supplies and the air we breathe have reached into and touched upon every corner of our daily lives.

A medical problem that has recently produced a great deal of public alarm is the dreaded disease, AIDS. We see AIDS everywhere — even on our beaches where offensive piles of hospital garbage, used syringes, decaying umbilical cords, diseased organs, bloody gauze pads and intravenous tubes — threaten our health. Anyone who would swim in such festering waters well might fear contraction of AIDS and a host of other diseases. For the very first time, man faces a predicament which may wind up destroying his total environment.

For nearly three centuries, the struggle to probe the nature of existence and resolve life's apparent paradoxes and problems has increasingly been considered the exclusive province of specialists. Questions as to the "how and why" of things are relinquished to the scientists, physicians, lawyers, engineers, analysts and artisans.

One may argue, this is, after all, the age of specialization. With so much knowledge in the world and so much information, how can the "common man" compete with the experts, who have advanced degrees, generous grants and banks of computers? The ordinary, unspecialized citizen must make do with seemingly obsolete equipment, reason, intuition, and raw instinct.

Could it be that the experts, in whom we have placed our absolute faith and trust, have, in certain respects, been acting under a crude illusion? The continuing hostility and dissension among the ranks of the specialists, authorities, and staunch defenders of so-called higher learning should go a long way toward providing evidence in favor of this point of view.

Today, as perhaps at no other time in our history, we are relinquishing a divinely inspired privilege. While science explores the vast reaches of space and invades the privacy even of the smallest subatomic particles, the individual's inborn imperative to probe the depths of mystical experience drifts like a ghost ship on a dark sea. The ship is the imprisoned human psyche, enslaved by a dying god, Progress. The sea is the ocean of illusion that we mistake for reality in this modern high-tech world.

The Zohar predicts that all inhabitants of planet Earth will one day come to grips with the profound mysteries of our cosmos and the many problems confronting mankind. No longer will man be forced to bow to the wisdom of experts, scientists and authorities who live in rarified intellectual atmosphere, beyond the reach of the mainstream of humanity. On that blessed day, in what has become known as the Age of Aquarius, the individual will again seize control of his sense of wonder and inquisitiveness, and, thus armed, regain a thorough knowledge of the exact nature of the universe and each person's place in it.

Here, the Zohar reveals the dynamic interplay and interconnectedness of our universe and man's relationship to it:

> For there is not a member in the human body that does not have its counterpart in the world as a whole. For as man's body consists of members and parts of various ranks, all acting and reacting upon each other so as to form one organism, so does the world at large consist of a hierarchy of created things, which when they properly act and react upon each other form one organic body.[1]

The preceding Zohar stresses the intimate connection between man and the cosmos, the constant conscious and unconscious interaction between the celestial kingdom and our mundane realm. As seen by the Zohar, the human body is a reflection of the vast cosmos. Human organs and limbs mirror the dynamics of an interstellar dance that is ever present in the universe.

The Zohar abounds with references to the role of man in achieving a mastery of his destiny. How utterly unlike the Zohar, which states that whoever makes use of the cosmic code, the Bible, supports the world and enables each part to perform its function, is the following Mishnaic declaration:

Know from where you cometh: from a decadent drop; where are you going: to a place of dust, worms and maggots.[2]

Dust, worms, and maggots indeed!

As portrayed by the Zohar, man is a spiritual entity whose fate is determined by the nature of his thoughts and actions. Rather than a rigid adherence to dogmatic doctrine, Kabbalah places religion in a context of spiritual experience. Man's corporeal body should not be treated as mere flesh and bones; the infinite aspect, the eternal soul, must be considered as well.

Genesis I declares that man was created on the sixth day of the Lord's creative process.[3] Why, asks the Zohar, was the creation of man saved for last? Because he is the culmination of all that preceded. In addition to being mere participators in the cosmic scheme, man, according to the Zohar, was given the role of determiner of universal and galactic activity.

One of the key elements of the Zoharic world view, one might almost say the essence of it, is the idea of assisting mankind toward an awareness of the unity and mutual interconnectedness of all aspects and events, so as to achieve a state of consciousness in which everything is perceived as being inseparable from the single all-pervading cosmic unity. To consciously perceive and embrace the union of all of the universe's myriad manifestations is to experience the highest reality.

Explorations into the subatomic world in the twentieth century have helped to reveal the dynamic interplay within the cosmic unity. From the kabbalistic perspective, the fundamental importance of these new scientific findings is that they provide a framework for achieving altered states of consciousness through which all separate manifestations are experienced as components in a vast intimate and integrated continuum. Kabbalah provides the mental and emotional apparatus needed to attain an elevated awareness of the interconnectedness of past, present and future, space, time and motion.

> The great kabbalist, Rabbi Hiyah, discoursing on the verse, "The blossoms appear on earth, the time of song has come, and the voice of the turtle dove is heard in our land,"[4] said that when the Lord created the universe, He endowed the earth with all the potential energy[5] required for it, but it did not spring forth until the appearance of man. It was only after man was created that all the products that were latent in the earth surfaced above ground. Likewise, the heavens did not impart strength to the earth until man appeared. For, as the Bible tells us, "All the plants were not yet on earth, the herbs of the field had not yet sprung up, the Lord had not caused it to rain upon the earth, for there was no man to till the ground."[6]

All the products of the earth remained hidden in its inner recesses, the heavens refrained from pouring rain upon the earth, because man had not yet been created. When man appeared the flowers grew, all of the earth's latent powers became revealed, in other words, "the time of song had come."[7]

The idea that man's internal activities can determine external events, indeed that man's thoughts influence and are inseparable from the external world, is a fiber woven throughout all sections of the Zohar. A key element of the Zoharic world view, is the idea that man is master of his destiny.[8] A similar view is expressed in the Bible:

> I call heaven and earth to witness against you this day that I have set before thee life and death, the blessing and the curse; therefore, choose life, that thou mayest live, thou and thy seed.[9]

Here the Bible promises that if the individual chooses life over death, control over his destiny is assured. The Bible stresses the fundamental interaction between the creation of the world, its history, and the creation and development of man. The idea of interconnectedness is central in establishing a conceptual nexus between the creation of the world and its future perfection to be brought about by the efforts of man.[10]

Of some concern to the author of the Zohar, as well as other commentators on the Bible, is the phrase, "I call heaven and earth to witness against you this day." Why, questioned the Zohar, is it necessary that the Lord retain heaven and earth as witness against the people? Why is there a necessity to witness man's positive or negative activity, when all is known to the Lord?

More confusion greets the reader of Rabbi Elazar's discourse on the text: "Lift up your eyes on high and see; who (Mi) hath created these?"[11] Lift up your eyes on high, to which place? To that place to which all eyes are turned, to wit, the eye opener. For by doing so we will "know the mysterious Ancient One, whose essence can be sought, but not found."[12]

For the reader of this Zohar, if its teachings in general seem abstruse, this passage is totally confusing. We are told to lift our eyes to seek the essence of the mysterious all-embracing Force, only to be told that its essence cannot be found.

*Mi*, the Hebrew word mentioned in Isaiah is a code for the extremity of heaven which is beyond the scope of human inquiry. Though the Force is ever to be sought its essence lays beyond our comprehension. There is, however, a lower extremity which is known by its code name *Mah* (what). The difference between the two is this. Although *Mi* is the real subject of inquiry, after a person, through inquiry and reflection, has reached the limit of knowledge he stops at *Mah* (what), as if to ask, what do I now know, what have my searchings achieved? At such times everything is as baffling as it was at the beginning.

The rewards of such investigation are alluded to in the verse where it is written, "I, Mah, have testified against thee, ..."[13] When the Temple was destroyed a voice went forth and said: "I, Mah, have testified against thee day by day from the days of old, as it is written I called heaven and earth to witness this day against you.[14] I, Mah, likened myself to you. I crowned you with holy crowns, and made you ruler over the earth."[15]

What emerges from the foregoing Zohar is the concept of witness as a code for instilling the Force and rulership within mankind. While the mysteries surrounding the all-embracing Force remain beyond our comprehension, man is indeed capable of understanding that which takes place in the lower extremity of inquiry, where the Force becomes manifested. It is here, in the lower phase of existence, that man is endowed with the power of rulership; it is here that full knowledge of how the Force directs and manifests can be achieved.

Without knowing that he was virtually paraphrasing the Zohar, the great physicist, Albert Einstein once eloquently defined the role of man in the cosmic scheme:

A human being is a part of the whole, called by us "universe", a part limited in time and space. He experiences himself, his thoughts and feelings as something separated from the rest — a kind of optical delusion of his consciousness. This delusion is a kind of prison for us, restricting us to our personal desires and to affection for a few persons nearest to us. Our task must be to free ourselves from this prison by widening our circle of compassion to embrace all living creatures and the whole nature in its beauty.

All things are connected. It is only those who through a lack of restriction doom themselves to lives of unhappiness and uncertainty. We each embrace a wealth of possibilities, including the potential to create or avert disasters; to remain static or to travel at the speed of thought; to dwell like trolls in dark caves of illusion and darkness, or break through to a world of light. Through the application of kabbalistic principles, we learn to transcend negative influences and claim our fair measure of personal and cosmic control.

*does Kabbalah release us from the prison of limitation?*

THE SOUL IS THAT ESSENCE OF A HUMAN BEING WHICH IS PART of the Whole, or universe. The feeling of separation that most of us experience is, as Einstein told us, a prison, an "optical delusion," which restricts us to a narrow range of personal desires. A further and more severe penalty for limiting ourselves to the physical realm is the extreme limitations imposed upon us by space and time.

Einstein suggests that our task must be to free ourselves from this prison by widening our circle of compassion to embrace all other living creatures. A noble suggestion indeed. Exactly how we are to free ourselves from this prison is not indicated.

How do we go about making these important and decisive changes in our lives?

All of us can cite examples of some action we took which seemed sensible in the beginning but led in the end to a less than positive result. Often we go against the grain of our natural inclinations to do what common sense dictates, only to discover that our natural instincts were right. Common sense, it seems, has an almost hypnotic quality. It lulls us into following it down the proverbial garden path and just when we are smelling the flowers of what we thought were our correct decisions we fall into a hole at the bottom of which is a metaphorical alligator or a sharp stick. Common sense is a trap into which many of us fall.

Just as the principles of Kabbalah cannot be perceived by the five common senses, neither can logic, reason and common sense lead us to the source of the river of our being. This is not to imply that common sense and logic do not have their place, for they do. It is only when logic, reason, and trial-and-error methods have failed us that we at last begin to understand that in spiritual matters the five common senses are not enough.

The purpose of Kabbalah is to remove the chains of logic and reason so that we may be released from the cage of our five common senses. For it is only by transcending the limits of these self-made linear boundaries that a direct link with the cosmic forces can be made. Only then can the real inner journey begin.

Rabbi Ashlag, the great twentieth-century kabbalist, philosopher, translator of the entire Zohar, and author the sixteen volume exposition on Lurianic Kabbalah, *Ten Luminous Emanations*, contended that breaking through to self awareness required only one prerequisite (a quality for which Rabbi Luria was obviously not lacking) and that prerequisite is desire.

It is said that when the Ari, Isaac Luria studied the Zohar, the flame of his desire burned so intensely that perspiration would quite literally pour off him.[1] Through his studies the Ari absorbed, converted, and transformed negativity (*klippot*) and thus became a channel for the *Or En Sof*, the Force. That his efforts were rewarded is evidenced by the fact that Lurianic Kabbalah has survived intact for over four centuries.

The Bible, in Deuteronomy, assures mankind the opportunity of transcending the robotic or lower level of consciousness which is ruled by the ego and the physical illusion. Instead of merely accepting the limitations with which we were born, the biblical code teaches us how to rise above physical, personal, and even celestial influences.

Abraham, the Patriarch, the world's first and foremost astrologer, was first named Abram. Abram saw in his chart that he would never beget a son with his wife Sarai. The Lord changed Abram's name to Abraham by the addition of the letter *Hay*. Likewise, the Lord removed the letter *Yod* from Sarai's name and placed in its stead the same letter *Hay*, thus changing the celestial influences and bringing about the birth of Isaac.[2]

This, of course, from a rational standpoint, is preposterous. How on earth could changing the letters of a name bring about the birth of a son? It simply does not make sense. In fact, celestial influences do not make sense, at least as that expression is commonly used. Indeed, utterly strange as it seems, the first step in elevating consciousness is to reject reason and common sense. For however well these paradigms of consciousness work for us in the physical world, they are impediments in the path to higher consciousness. Union with a higher order of reality cannot be taught, it cannot be thought, it cannot be bought, it has to be experienced.

For anyone who has entered the sanctuary of Kabbalah, the answers to life's problems and crisis can only be emphatic in the affirmative. In these fast-paced and fragmented times, bombarded as we are by sensory stimuli, what pleasure it gives one to enter the refuge of an ancient tradition that is at the same time so elemental and yet so complete. Here, where the mighty cult of progress holds no sway, we find a life-affirming doctrine that transcends the intellect without denying the Mind.

Through the study of Kabbalah we confirm what kabbalists have known for centuries, namely, that there is another invisible, all-pervading energy-intelligence, not unlike gravity or electromagnetism, that has yet to be scientifically substantiated. Moreover, and far more importantly, we learn to connect with that energy and make it part of our lives.

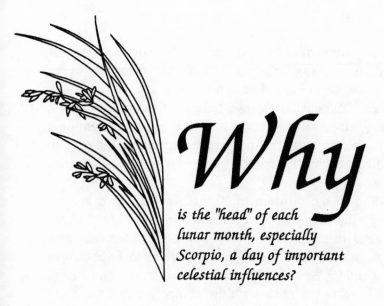

*Why* is the "head" of each lunar month, especially Scorpio, a day of important celestial influences?

IN A PREVIOUS CHAPTER ON COSMIC DANGER ZONES, WE explored the destructive aspects of Scorpio and the Hebrew month of Heshvan. Yet, despite its hallmark for misfortune, chaos and disorder, the first day, or *Rosh Hodesh*, of Heshvan is scored as the most supremely positive day of the year.

How can a constellation such as Scorpio possess the immense negative influence of devastation which manifested as the Deluge, yet contain within its cosmic framework a first day of such enormous power of positiveness?

We will examine the question of *Rosh Hodesh* (the first day of any lunar month influence) and more specifically the celestial influences leading up to the intensely positive *Rosh Hodesh* of Scorpio. First, however, in considering this question, it will be of benefit to briefly compare the conventional and kabbalistic astrological systems.

Both the conventional and the kabbalistic systems of astrology divide the twelve signs of the zodiac according to the four elements: earth, air, fire, and water. In conventional astrology, each element is represented by a further designation of Cardinal, Fixed, and Mutable. Unlike most conventional astrologers, the kabbalist astrologer has achieved a thorough understanding of why this is so.[1]

According to the wisdom of Kabbalah, the Force reveals itself through the four phases, represented in astrology as earth, air, water and fire. Yet, like everything else in the universe, astrology must also conform to what is known to Kabbalah as the Three Column System. These three "columns" (left, right and central) which correlate with the components of the atom (electron, proton, and neutron) reveal themselves in every word, every particle of matter, every thought, deed and event, every action, reaction, and interaction in our universe.

The Force manifests on earth in strict accordance with these three divisions. Thus each of the four elements or phases is imbued with a predominance of one of the three columns, namely: the right column Desire to Share, manifested in water signs; the left column Desire to Receive, symbolized by the fire signs; and the central column Desire to Restrict, as portrayed by the air signs.

For example, of the three fire signs, Aries represents the right column or major force of fire's energy-intelligence; Leo represents the left column; while Sagittarius displays the attributes of the central column of the fire force.

The fact that all energy and life expresses itself in the physical world according to the three column system, however, does not in any way negate or compromise the Force's unity. This primal life flow is directed and filtered through many diverse expressions of consciousness, thus establishing infinite layers of energy-intelligences, but it is but one single Force expressing itself in an endless multitude of forms and patterns. The three columns are expressions of the all-prevailing Force of One.

Only when a unit of energy is physically expressed does it become directed by the three column system and become a part of the particular earthly vessel in which it is contained. Free flowing atoms in space are in a physically potential state. But once contained in a wall or table, the same atoms become manifested in a different, more physically "active" form. The earth signs make atoms appear as solid objects. Captured by an earth sign, an atom becomes active energy.

Different frames of reference determine an atomic unit's, behavior. When contained within water all three components of the three column system act according to the intelligence of sharing, expansion, or extension. It is, however, possible for each of the three components to express itself independently of the others, albeit always within the intelligence framework of water.[2]

Returning to Scorpio, the kabbalists designate her position as the fire, left column or negative energy-intelligent force of water. The internal character of water is one of positivity, sharing and outpouring.[2] Thus, each of the three water signs (Scorpio, Pisces and Cancer) must function and express itself within the framework of water and its intrinsic characteristic of positivity.

The question that should be raised at this time, is how can the kabbalists establish a negative water sign? This idea seems to run counter to the essential idea of water intelligence which expresses itself in a positive manner. Water seeks its own level. "Why?" asks the Kabbalist. The answer is that all physical entities are governed by thought-energy-intelligences, and water's energy-intelligence is one of sharing or extension.

This revolutionary idea has long been understood by the kabbalist. His interpretation of the atom enables us to better understand the world around us. All energy and intelligent life forms come from and are motivated by the one basic manifestation of life, the Force. This primal life flow is directed and filtered through many diverse expressions of consciousness, thus establishing infinite layers of energy-intelligences. Yet it is but one single Force expressing itself in an endless multitude of forms and patterns.

More fully expressed, this means that the Force reveals itself through a continuum of events by which man may experience the wellspring of this creation. The Force reveals itself through four essential energy-intelligences. They are the Desire to Share manifested in water signs, the Desire to Receive, symbolized by the fire signs, and the Central Column, or Desire to Restrict, portrayed by the air signs. These three energy-intelligences form the core of any and all arrangements of the Force. The three forces operate by the same pattern in all structures, from the tiniest atom to the greatest unit of the cosmos. One set of universal laws pervades and unifies all of the intelligent life force in the cosmos.

A unit of force like the atom does not become expressed unless physically manifested. When a unified whole of energy

is contained within a vessel, when its energy circuit —
containing the three phases of desire — is physically expressed,
the fourth dimension, referred to as earth, becomes the dominant
and prevailing force. The unit is now directed by the particular
earth quality in which it is contained.

An earth sign makes atoms appear as solid objects. Atoms
flowing freely through space would not prevent one's hand from
passing through them. But once contained in a wall or table, the
atoms, which make up and take up 99% of the table or wall,
become an active force. In space, the atoms are merely a
potential form of energy. Captured by an earth sign, they
become active energy.

What seems to emerge from the foregoing is that frames of
reference determine the atomic unit's behavior. When contained
within water all three components behave in the intelligence of
sharing, expansion or extension. However, the three components
each have an opportunity to express themselves independently
of each other, albeit within the framework of water intelligence.

How does the left, or negative, column of water intelligence
express itself? Simply by overexpansion, overextension or too
much sharing. In the form of water, a surplus results in
flooding. Too much sharing by a parent spoils a child. A
business expanding too rapidly too soon may result in failure.

The month of Scorpio follows upon the heels of the month
of Libra when the awesome power of the Force becames a
manifested state of expression. This is necessary so as to
provide humankind with a sufficient life force energy to last for
a full year.

During the month of Libra the Force begins to make manifest our cosmic blueprint for the coming year. This is the month in which the old celestial energy pattern reaches the end of its cycle and the next year's pattern is established. The month of Libra brings with it a tremendous outpouring of energy, enough to carry us through to the following year. This is not to say that the outcome and future of one's destiny in the coming year is entirely predetermined. Each of us has the ability to influence and even radically alter the nature of our lives and environment.[3]

This metaphysical changing of the guard, which begins on the *Rosh Hodesh*, the first day of Libra, and culminates on the *Rosh Hodesh* of Scorpio, reveals itself in a variety of ways. The strong sense of disconnectedness felt by many of us on the first day of Libra is the result of this change in what we might call the metaphysical DNA. Throughout the month of Libra, the Force gradually establishes itself, building, growing, becoming stronger until it is released in its full spendor on the *Rosh Hodesh* of Scorpio.

The Holy (read Wholly) days of Succoth were established to provide us with a cosmic timetable when all of mankind could establish the Light of Hasadim (Mercy).

The Light of Hasadim is a code contained within the lexicon of kabbalistic language. The Force, also referred to by its coded name, Light of Wisdom, must be enclosed and concealed within the Light of Hasadim (Mercy) for it to become revealed. The paradox of revealment or manifestation of the Force (energy) lies precisely in the ability of the vessel or Hasadim to conceal the energy.

Consider the plus and minus poles of a light bulb that jointly provide the revealment and manifestation of electricity. They are, in effect, two opposing forces that together provide a unified expression of the all-embracing whole, the Force. Why must there be a positive pole in the light bulb when in fact it is the negative pole that draws the current? Because the positive pole provides the proper setting for the Force to become physically expressed. The positive pole, with its intrinsic energy-force, the Light of Hasadim, furnishes the energy-force, providing expansion and extension. Light of Hasadim is the kabbalistic code name for a positive pole force.

The Light of Hasadim, also referred to as the positive vessel, ultimately makes manifest the Force. While the negative pole draws the current towards the receptacle, it is nevertheless the positive pole with its Light of Hasadim, that provides the glowing expression of the bulb when drawn through the central column or restriction of the filament. When all of humankind, jointly and as an integrated whole, make manifest the whole of cosmic Hasadim on Succoth, the flow and manifestation of the Force to provide the life force for all of earth's inhabitants is indeed staggering. This might be compared to a dam suddenly having its floodgates opened. The onrushing waters could bring on flooding and havoc.

Consequently, the Zodiac sign of Scorpio, following the release of humankind's absorption of an astounding supply of energy, finds itself in a predicament. The cosmic force of Hasadim's sudden release into the cosmos is responsible for the enormous negative behavior of this water sign. Scorpio is the effect of this phenomena and not the cause of it.

Hasadim, portrayed by water in our physical universe, provides and extends the life force of the Lord to all of Earth's inhabitants. That is an enormous quantity of energy suddenly making its appearance on the stage of Earth's orchestration.

For a few spiritually powerful souls beginning new ventures in the month of Scorpio it is appropriate and indeed advantageous. They are to be encouraged to go to all lengths, sparing no efforts in new ventures. However, for the majority of us, it is most advisable that we refrain from making any decisions concerning new ventures during the month of Scorpio. All of the foregoing concerns the entire lunar month of Scorpio with the exception of the first day of this month.

The first day, *Rosh Hodesh*, the top of any month contains a unique quality within its cosmic frame. Being the first day, it symbolizes the power of *Keter* (Crown). Like a seed there exists within *Rosh Hodesh* the potential for roots, leaves, branches and blossoms and fruit.

The answer to the mystery surrounding Rosh Hodesh is provided by the Zohar.[4] The mystical significance of Rosh Hodesh was well known to all ancient cultures. Temples, monuments, and religious teachings stand as testimonials to the influence believed to have been exercised by the heavens over the daily lives of men. The ordered external structure of the cosmos was thought to symbolize the metaphysical workings of the celestial realm.

It is written that the Lord, the Force, goes with Jacob the Patriarch on each and every Rosh Hodesh. Jacob, the central column energy-intelligence, is called *Mamre*, indicating the awesome power emerging from this union. And only when the forces were in balance did the heavens declare their majesty and influence. According to the Zohar, the Force, accompanied and channeled by the energy-intelligence of Jacob, becomes manifest as a unifying force on Rosh Hodesh.

According to kabbalistic interpretation, Rosh Hodesh indicates the emergence of the central column which unites the two opposing energy-intelligences of the Force, namely the Desire to Share and the Desire to Receive. The conductor between these opposing forces is the energy-intelligence of restriction, indicated by the code-name, Jacob. When restriction takes place, meaning that the Force is kept from entering the vessel which is possessed of the energy-intelligence of Desire to Receive, the result is an explosion by which is revealed the immensely positive energy-intelligence of Desire to Share.

This is the condition before the appearance of the new moon. All systems are ready and waiting for the moment when the switch will be turned to the "on" position. When the energy-intelligence of a particular lunar month appears, the Force illuminates the heavens in a colossal explosion and the vibrating web of life's ceaseless motion begins its cosmic dance anew.

The universe has been programmed to evolve in the series of twelve months toward its final emendation. The Zohar points out that the behavior and orientation of any Rosh Hodesh is an encapsulated energy-intelligence which bursts forth from the Cosmos, seeding the universe like a cosmic egg.

The Force of the Lord begins to reveal its ruling power on Rosh Hodesh, triggered by the particular sign of the Zodiac. Consequently, maintains the Zohar, the dimension of light and power provided by Rosh Hodesh permits human control over individual destiny. There is no conflict between determinism and free will.

"The Lord created one against the other,"[5] declares King Solomon. The *Tsimtsum*, the first restriction, created a situation such that the predictive laws of the cosmos and free will could exist side by side. The negative intelligence of the constellation is pitted against the positive structure of Force. The negative aspect relies on the postive for its sustenance, the postive depends on the negative for its revealment.

King Solomon appears to offer humankind a unique ability to penetrate and influence the structural reality of the universe in a way undreamed of in the days of Newton. It is not the purpose of this book to delve deeply into the kabbalistic concept of opposite forces. This subject is dealt with elsewhere. Yet it should be rememered that the duality of free will and determinism is a key element in the cosmic process.

The Zohar emphasizes direct and intimate consciousness of the celestial, metaphysical realm.[6] Rosh Hodesh is a day, which, though often charaterized as a dogmatic ritual commanded by the Bible, can provide us with a connection with the awesome power of the Force. Connecting with this power establishes for us a month of pure positive consciousness.

Most of us are trapped in a narrow frame of reference that severely limits our human potential. Scorpio's Rosh Hodesh offers a unique opportunity for blessings and continuity, which, on this day alone, can release us from our self-imposed imprisonment. This is precisely the concept presented by the Zohar.[7]

Rabbi Shimon spoke on the verse: "And Thou, O Lord, be not far from me: O my strength, hasten Thou to help me."[8]

Said he, (Rabbi Shimon): "The two invocations, Thou and Lord represent *Malkhut* and *Tifereth*, respectively." Two worlds, one of illusion (Malkhut) and the other of reality (Tifereth), Lord is the Tetragrammaton, Thou refers to *Malkhut*. The Psalmist prayed that the two worlds would become united. For when the one separates from the other, all light is darkened and removed from the world.

Our universe receives its beneficence, nourishment, and positive energy by way of *Malkhut*. She (Malkhut) acts as a satellite for channeling the awesome power of the Force to mankind. When Malkhut, which is the lower light (Malkhut is the kabbalistic code name for the moon's internal energy intelligence), does not receive the Force from *Tifereth*, she has nothing to offer this universe. For this reason, the Temple (the energy conductor for the Force) was destroyed in the period of Jeremiah. Humankind caused a severance in the cosmic connection between *Tifereth* and *Malkhut*. Although the Second Temple was built, the Force did not return as before.

What seems to emerge from the preceding Zohar is the duality that is present in all energy-intelligent activity. The Zohar drives home the point that if negative human activity prevails, then a severance between energy (Tifereth) and matter (Malkhut) seems to take place. This separation, which manifests at all levels, from the cosmos down to the realm of subatomic activity, is the result of mankind's invasion of the cosmic bond between the forces of *Tifereth* and *Malkhut*.

Thus, the illusionary disintegration of matter, the horrors of uncertainty, the process of discontinuity set into the lifestyle of Earth's environment. However, let us not forget for one moment that a parallel universe exists which maintains its connection with continuity and fulfillment, where the joy of certainty never ceases.

On Rosh Hodesh there is no severance between Tifereth and Malkhut. One needs only to be aware of the significance of Rosh Hodesh and then tap its enormous energy — more so on Scorpio's Rosh Hodesh when an incredible release of the Force takes place. On Rosh Hodesh, the entire potential of Scorpio reveals itself. The advantage enjoyed by Scorpio does not, on Rosh Hodesh, present itself in a negative manner. Because of its "potential" nature, the manifested state of Scorpio's enormous negative behavior does not affect Rosh Hodesh.

Thankfully, humankind cannot in any way alter the cosmic realm. We are given only the choice of whether or not to connect with and thus tap its awesome power. The tools, methodology and channels are provided by which we can enhance our future physical and mental well-being. The Holy (read Wholly) days of Succoth were established to provide us with a cosmic timetable when we all can establish a link with the Light of Hasadim (Mercy).

The friendly cosmos extends itself from the first day of each month to the fifteenth day of each lunar month. Of course, this cosmic period does not include those unfriendly months mentioned previously. Given the proper attitude of restriction, we can tap Rosh Hodesh's awesome power and not fear the consequences that one may incur during any other day of

Scorpio. Therefore, the first day of lunar Scorpio is a most beneficial day to begin new ventures.

# How

*does the knowledge of the power of cosmic energy improve our awareness?*

ANOTHER DAY OF IMMENSE COSMIC POWER IS THE FIFTEENTH day of lunar Leo. It is no coincidence that Leo, a month that witnessed the fiery destruction of two Holy Temples, should contain a day of such enormous cosmic energy.

Predominantly joyful in Temple times, lunar Leo's character became increasingly somber after Rome's destruction of the Temple. As more and more catastrophes occurred, the cosmic energy of this period became increasingly restricted, as evidenced by the Mishnaic adage, "When Av comes in, gladness is diminished."[1]

Like Scorpio, lunar Leo, too, is a month of immense power. The difference between them is that Scorpio, being a water sign, manifested its power of devastation in the flood, whereas Leo, a fire sign, expressed its awesome power of destruction in the burning of the Holy Temples.

It is this destructive aspect of lunar Leo which makes it a month not generally conducive to beginning new ventures. Being a fire sign, Leo represents a time of overheating and explosive negative energy. The intensity of the Force during this month is such that the majority of people are incapable of channeling its unpredictable energy. The sun is capable of creating the "Greenhouse Effect."

However, the celestial blueprint, thankfully, did in temple times and continues today to provide breathing spaces within cosmic danger zones. Such a time is the fifteenth day of lunar Leo. Indeed, Rabbi Shimon Ben Gamliel said that there never were in Israel greater days of joy than the fifteenth day of the month of Av and Yom Kippur. On the fifteenth day of Av the daughters of Jerusalem came out and danced in the vineyards exclaiming at the same time, "Young man, lift up thine eyes and see what thou chooses for thyself. Do not set thine eyes on beauty but set thine eyes on family."[2]

The Zohar tells us: "On this day (Rosh Hashana) the moon is concealed and it does not shine until the tenth day, when Israel turns with a perfect repentance, so that Binah (the energy store) gives light to her (Moon). Hence this day is called the day of Atonements (plural), because two lights are shedding the Light of the Force, since the higher light (*Binah*) is illumining the lower (*Malkhut*). For on this day the moon receives illumination from Binah and not from the sun (*Ze'ir Anpin*).[3] Therefore, Malkhut does not illumine until Yom Kippur."[4]

In the Zohar's description of Yom Kippur,[5] one senses an intimacy between man and the cosmos, rather than merely the recounting of a detailed religious doctrine. What underlies and penetrates the Zoharic interpretation of the Holy Days is the enormous power of the Force which prevails on those days.

The moon depends on the sun for her sustenance. And since her energy reaches Malkhut indirectly through Ze'ir Anpin (sun), the potency is greatly diminished. However, on Yom Kippur, Malkhut's (the moon's) energy connects directly with the energy storehouse of Binah, and her power becomes similar to the infinite energy of the sun.[6] Thus, when the Talmud compares the fifteenth of Av with Yom Kippur, it does so because tremendous celestial energy is revealed on this day.

With this perspective in mind, the once confusing section of the Talmud now under consideration suddenly comes alive. "On these days the daughters of Jerusalem came out and danced..." indicates the elevated consciousness reached by the daughters of Jerusalem as a result of this infusion of celestial energy. The expression "set thine eyes on family" refers to the union of the lower Hay of the Tetragrammaton (Malkhut) becoming united on the fifteenth day of Av, with *Binah*, the upper Hay of the Tetragrammaton, thus becoming one united family. It is on this day, the fifteenth day of Av, when the energies of Ze'ir Anpin and *Malkhut*, the Sun and the Moon, unite, creating a most powerful and beneficial force within our cosmos.[7]

The fifteenth day of any lunar month is a perfect day to begin new ventures, (excluding, of course, those months falling within the Cosmic Danger Zones). This holds true for the lunar month of Leo as well.

The Bible, Talmud and Zohar are not documents for religion, but instruments, mediums by which we can achieve lives and societies free of chaos, drugs, crime, hatred and animosity. The Talmud just cited does not address itself merely to Israel or the daughters of Jerusalem. The sages of the Talmud provide information to assist all of mankind towards achieving joy and contentment.

The universe is a cosmic code, which it is the Zohar's task to decipher. Revealed through this cosmic code is a celestial order beyond man's immediate rational experience. Despite billions spent on space travel, we remain in darkness when it comes to understanding the internal nature of cosmic energies. The Zohar exposes the existence of the forces that shape the human condition and exert their control over our physical universe. More importantly, it shows us how to use them.

On the fifteenth of Av, *Malkhut*, meaning our physically manifested universe, taps its energy directly from Binah, the energy storehouse. Throughout the year, her energy supply depends upon her position with the sun, drawing her (Malkhut's) sustenance by way of *Ze'ir Anpin* (sun). Therefore the Zohar recommends the start of new ventures during the first half of any lunar month, and not during the second half. The first half of any given month sees an infusion of energy within our cosmos, whereas the second half experiences a decrease in cosmic beneficence. Hence the gradual increase in the moon's luminosity during the first fifteen days, and its gradual reduction to nothing at the end of the month.

By mating directly with the *Binah* consciousness, *Malkhut* (Moon) achieves an indirect intimacy with the immense intelligent energy of *Hokhmah* (Wisdom). Once Malkhut succeeds in a cosmic connection with the exalted level of Hokhmah, then she is in a state of communication with the Force.[8] This occurs without any intervention on the part of mankind. All that is necessary to tap the immense energy of the fifteenth day of Av is knowledge of the celestial patterns and forces which have been arranged by the cosmic blueprint for the benefit of all mankind.

Unlike the fifteenth of Av, *Yom Kippur* requires a substantial effort on the part of each individual in order to elevate his consciousness to a state of communion with Binah consciousness.[9] Before any connection can have the desired effect, the individual must first strive to transform his own Desire to Receive for the Self Alone to a Desire to Receive for the Sake of Sharing.

Our future depends on our actions. We can control our lives and our destinies or not, depending on whether we choose to activate the restrictive mechanism necessary for the removal of Bread of Shame or indulge in the Desire to Receive for Oneself Alone. Selfish activity creates a program of uncertainty and fragmentation, in which even the most seemingly flawless plans become subject to quantum indecision. Unselfish activity, on the other hand, removes all the rough edges and replaces any doubts or uncertainty with Blessings. Through positive consciousness we can re-format our cosmic blueprint and bring peace, certainty, and immense energy to our lives.[10]

There are several spiritual paths by which the metaphysical universe may be experienced. Each involves varying levels of consciousness and each provides a connection with cosmic energy fields that can increase our awareness and improve our well-being. Such connections are particularly needed today when our environment has become so polluted with affliction.

Having ascended the spiritual ladder, which means achieving tikune and correcting the faults and flaws of prior incarnations, one achieves a new level of consciousness that allows him to dictate the path he will take throughout his lifetime. Such an individual has, in fact, changed the cosmic pattern of his or her life.

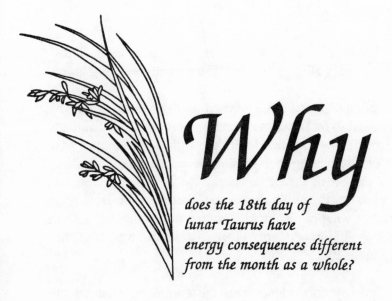

# Why

*does the 18th day of
lunar Taurus have
energy consequences different
from the month as a whole?*

A PREVIOUS CHAPTER CAUTIONED THE READER TO AVOID LUNAR
Taurus, a month of abstention and traditional mourning customs,
when contemplating new ventures. Yet the eighteenth day of
lunar Taurus is a day when new ventures have a high
probability of success. That the eighteenth should be so
regarded is strange, for this is when 24,000 students of Rabbi
Akiva were tortured and put to death because they did not
sufficiently honor one another.[1]

Taurus and Scorpio have much in common. Both are months
of universal negative energy, yet both contain days of immense
positive energy. Moreover, of all the signs of the Zodiac, they
alone have been given additional names. Scorpio acquired the
Hebrew name "Bul," which points to the idea of exactness, "on
target" or "right on," appropriate for Scorpio's internal energy-
intelligence; Taurus has the distinctive pre-exilic name "Ziv,"[2]

meaning "brightness" or "light." It is this attribute of "light" which is both the challenge of lunar Taurus and its saving grace.

The challenge faced by Taureans is their tendency to be complacent and to feel always correct in their position. Taureans feel comfortable — connected with the light — no matter how disastrous or devastating their circumstances. It is quite futile to attempt to punish or "teach a lesson" to a Taurean who has wronged you. For they will always feel that the truth is on their side no matter what punishment is meted out to them. This can be a serious hindrance for those Taureans who are not spiritually inclined.

It was not by coincidence that the commencement of the Temple by King Solomon took place in the month of Taurus,[3] and that its completion occurred in the month of *Bul*, which is the eight month sign of *Heshvan* and Scorpio. These two months were carefully chosen by King Solomon to begin and end his endeavor. Make no mistake in considering the possibility that it was his building contractors who could not begin earlier, or who by chance completed its construction in the month of Bul!

King Solomon, the Wise, understood the cosmos and the methods by which to tap its power. Solomon knew that completing the Temple in the month of Scorpio (Bul-exactness) would provide an infusion of spiritual energy-intelligence sufficient to fuel the Temple for some four hundred years.

In their wisdom, the sages of the Talmud and Zohar realized that the all-knowing Force must have foreseen man's greed and mad race for power. And that certainly He must have known that the vast majority of the Earth's inhabitants, ensconced as we are in the Desire to Receive for Ourselves Alone, would be incapable of dealing with a large infusion of spiritual energy. Thus, He found the cosmos in a situation not unlike the situation in lunar Scorpio, which resolved itself in the Great Deluge.

In the case of Scorpio, the solution was to impregnate the universe with a positive energy sufficient to restrict the unlimited needs of the Desire to Receive. The day chosen was Rosh Hodesh. A similar infusion of positive energy was necessary to stabilize the enormous negative power of Taurus.

Rabbi Shimon Bar Yohai resolved the matter by departing this world on the eighteenth day of lunar Taurus.

"On the day that Rabbi Shimon Bar Yohai desired to leave this world, he prepared his final words. To all his friends gathered beside him, he revealed new esoteric mysteries and teachings." Rabbi Abba, who was present on this occasion, reported that the Light emanating from Rabbi Shimon was so intense that he could not approach him.[4]

To the reader, the Zoharic description of Rabbi Shimon Bar Yohai's departure may sound like a story out of fairyland. Such, however, was the power of a man who had transcended the limitations of time, space and motion. It is significant that the day chosen by Rabbi Shimon to leave this world was the eighteenth day of Taurus.[5]

Regarding the eighteenth day of lunar Taurus, the Ari, Isaac Luria, in his discussion of this period (known by its code name *Sefirat ha Omer*), states that "this day is the revelation of compassion, by the mystery of the code name *Elokim Haim*, living Lord. An attachment with *Binah* consciousness takes place. This idea is revealed by another coded energy-intelligence known as the *Sefirah of Hod*."[6]

For nearly two thousand years, hundreds of thousands of pilgrims have made the journey to the small hamlet in the Galilee known as Meron, some to pay tribute, others to pray for Rabbi Shimon's intervention and support for their well being. A handful take advantage of Rabbi Shimon's return to earthly existence on this day of the 18th of Iyar and draw upon his channelling of the Force.

The Zohar points to the enormous power of Taurus in its discussion on the Tabernacle:

It is written: "And the Lord spoke unto Moses in the wilderness of Sinai in the Tabernacle in the first day of the second month, etc."[7] The Revelation on Mont Sinai correlates with the power of the sun (*Ze'ir Anpin*), the Tabernacle to the moon (*Malkhut*). This second month is called Ziv, an allusion to the unusual circuitry between Ze'ir Anpin (Sun) and Malkhut (Moon), when the worlds altogether found themselves in grand unification.[8]

The extrinsic and somewhat unruly atmosphere of this extremely high-powered time provides fair warning to those who are incapable of dealing with such a huge infusion of celestial energy. Yet, spiritually minded individuals are strongly advised to begin a new venture on the eighteenth day of lunar Taurus, for success is all but assured.

With Kabbalah we establish continuity and freedom from doubt by revealing the inner sanctum of the cosmos and by tapping its energy for the benefit and well-being of all mankind.

*The heavens declare the glory of the Lord, and the firmament showeth his handiwork. Day unto day uttereth speech, and night unto night revealeth knowledge. There is no speech, there are no words, neither is their voice heard. Their line is gone out through all the earth, and their words to the end of the world. In them he hath set a tent for the sun.* **Psalms, 19 : 1 - 5**

# *Why*

*is lunar Aquarius*
*a proptious time to*
*begin new ventures?*

IN THEIR QUEST TO UNCOVER THE UNDERLYING PATTERNS AND causes which express themselves in celestial movements and events, kabbalists have arrived at many conclusions which scientists deem absurd. The kabbalist, for example, maintains that the world is an illusion, that light has no speed, and that the stars and planets are not mindless in their monthly cycles. Indeed, far from being the dark, unfriendly, and chaotic environment proposed by science, the kabbalist sees the cosmos as a reflection of himself.

It is hardly surprising that given the same basic materials, scientists and kabbalists should have arrived at such vastly different conclusions. Their working methods are diametrically opposed. The scientist asks "how," the kabbalist asks "why?"; the scientist works from the outside in, the kabbalist from the inside out; the scientist divides the world into that which is animate and that which is inanimate, living and dead, while the kabbalist proceeds on the assumption that because the Creator, who is the epitome of aliveness, is everywhere, it follows that everything, a rock, a tree, a man, must of necessity be permeated with a level and frame of intelligent consciousness.

Another essential difference between the world view of the kabbalist and that of the scientist, is that the scientist attempts to distance himself from that which he is analyzing, while the kabbalist, realizing that everyone and everything are interconnected, understands that one cannot study something outside of oneself without also studying oneself. True objectivity is impossible. It is futile to look at something outside of oneself without including oneself in the equation — the observer and the observed are one and the same.

The universe is us.

With this in mind, let us examine why the month of lunar Aquarius is such a propitious time to begin new ventures, especially the fifteenth day of the lunar month.

The reader is by now familiar with the kabbalistic world view that celestial bodies are positioned in the cosmos according to their own particular energy-intelligence and aspect of desire to receive. And that their placement in the cosmos can provide us with a glimpse of the internal structure of the Force and of ourselves.

When two signs of the zodiac form an angle of 180 degrees they are considered in opposition. Each of the twelve signs of the zodiac has its opposite, a sign with which it forms a natural polarity and balance. Leo, a fire sign, and Aquarius, an air sign, are in direct opposition. Aquarius occupies the fire position in the last region of the zodiac, Leo is situated within the fire position of the second region. Taurus and Scorpio, representing earth and water respectively, are also in opposition, as are Aries and Libra, representing fire and air. Other signs in opposition are Gemini and Sagittarius, air and fire; Cancer and Capricorn, water and earth; and Virgo and Pisces, earth and water.

Thus the fifteenth day of lunar Leo and the fifteenth day of lunar Aquarius are like two sides of the same coin: each is dependent upon and reveals the other. Like the poles of a magnet, when these two signs are at odds, they boldly assert their individuality, when they are in harmony they reveal the cosmic whole. Like all signs in opposition they have potential to bring out both the best and the worst in each other.

Aquarius is depicted in a kneeling position, his urn of living water resting on one shoulder as its contents spill out in front of him. The emblem of this eleventh sign is quite simple. Aquarius itself is derived from the Latin "aqua" meaning water. The urn portrays the Hebrew cosmic code of *Kad*, pitcher. The numerical value of Kad — which consists of two letters Kaf and Dalet — is twenty-four, a number revealed by many narrations of misfortune and death.

> And when Pinhas, the son of Elazar, the son of Aaron the High Priest saw it, he rose up from the midst of the congregation, and took a spear in his hand... So the plague was stayed from the children of Israel. And those that died by the plague were twenty-four thousand.[1]

An even more serious example of the *Kad* consciousness is portrayed by the Talmud's description of the destruction of the Holy Temple, where it is said that Rabbi Akiba had 12,000

of them died at the same time because "they did not treat each
other with respect." A Tanna (Sage) taught: All of them died
between Passover and Pentecost. Rabbi Hama ben Abbaor (or
it might be said, Rabbi Hiyah ben Abin) said: "All of them died
a cruel death."[2]

Yet the water which man shares from his Kad (urn) is the
water of knowledge and consciousness. Thus in the celestial
neighborhood associated with King David,[3] Aquarius is viewed
as sign with great conflict, water versus fire. The inclusion of
the Kad, the pitcher, represents the suffering and bloodshed that
will accompany and usher in the final stages of the Messiah.

Aquarius is associated with communication and is
synonymous with the age of Messiah, when the concept of
"Love thy Neighbor"[4] will prevail among all mankind. The
Zohar states[5] that "in the days of the Messiah, there will no
longer be the necessity for one to request of his neighbor, teach
me wisdom, for it is written: 'one day they will no longer teach
every man his neighbor and every man his brother, saying know
the Lord.' For they shall all know Me, from the youngest to the
oldest of them."[6]

The Hebrew letters and words are coded for the revelation
of energy-intelligence. Surprisingly enough, the Hebrew word
*Shevat* (the name of lunar Aquarius) has an Aramaic
counterpart, *Sharvit*.

For an interpretation of the significance of this let us turn to
the Zohar:

Rabbi Isaac opened a discourse on the verse: "and the remnant of Jacob shall be in the midst of many peoples as dew from the Lord, as showers upon the grass."[7] Observe that every day, as soon as day breaks, a certain female cosmic force awaits her mate for the cosmic connection to reveal the light of day that emanates from the Garden of Eden. Upon receiving the force of the three column energy-intelligence system[8] Sharvit (Shavit) rules as a scepter in maintaining balance in the universe.[9]

What emerges from the Zohar is the mystery of the internal force of lunar Aquarius. It is the energy force of the three column system, the Messiah consciousness, indicating the advent of the Messiah, along with its blessing of "Peace on earth, good will toward one's fellow man."[10]

The internal energy-intelligence of water is that of sharing. The fixed or middle position of Aquarius among the three signs — Capricorn, Aquarius and Pisces — brings to it a fire consciousness and therefore the *Kad* code. To this we now add the air consciousness symbolized by the concept of Messiah. We now see the Aquarian sign as an embodiment of central column energy-intelligence. Aquarius personifies the totality of the Force, with a consciousness of fire, water and air wrapped up in one all-embracing whole. Thus Aquarius provides mankind with a cosmic zone extremely beneficial for new ventures.[11]

With our new kabbalistic perspective of lunar Aquarius, we can now begin to understand the traditions that surround the fifteenth day of this month. *Tu B'Shevat*, the Hebrew name for the 15th of Aquarius, is the festival of the New Year of Trees.

For traditionalists, there is but one New Year, and that is Rosh Hashana. For the reader of kabbalistic material, the idea of a New Year for trees, animals, and vegetables should hardly be surprising.

Quantum physics concurs with the kabbalistic view of reality in the sense that both see matter (animate and inanimate) not as a passive and inert phenomenon, but rather as a dance of metaphysical patterns and tendencies, a vibrating rhythm integral to and inseparable from a cosmic complex which consists of space, time, energy, matter, and consciousness. The kabbalist makes a further distinction, placing all of these outward manifestations of the cosmic order under the direct influence of *Desire to Receive*.[12]

The Ari, Isaac Luria, taught that there are four basic realities of energy-intelligence in our mundane universe, namely, the "inanimate" reality, vegetation reality, animal reality, and the human reality.[13] These four realities are extensions of the four basic elements of water, fire, air and earth, which are themselves extensions of the four stimulations of the four aspects of Desire to Receive. The four stimulations or basic intelligences of the Desire to Receive are known by their code names: *Hesed* (Mercy); *Gevurah* (Judgment); *Tifereth* (Beauty); and *Malkhut* (Kingdom).[14]

Why does Kabbalah place such a premium on desire? Because as we penetrate reality from a kabbalistic perspective, we come to the inevitable realization that desire is the motivating force of the physical universe. In the dynamic world view of Kabbalah there is no place for stasis or purely material substance. All the basic elements in the universe, physical and metaphysical, are in fact powered by desire. Whether we are speaking of gravity, electromagnetism, organic growth, earthquakes, weather patterns, the actions of man, everywhere we look we see manifestations of desire.

The physical world is desire. Everything on earth is governed by desire. The difference between beings of a higher order and those of a lower is simply that the former possess greater Desire to Receive. Even the so-called inanimate kingdom is possessed of desire. Delve into the metaphysical reality of a rock and we find desire, albeit in a low degree.

Having spent more than three millenniums exploring the interrelatedness of man and his cosmos, kabbalists are unique among celestial investigators in providing a unified description of creation. Since the Golden Age of Safed, some four centuries ago, kabbalists have had a fully detailed metaphysical model of the universe. How did they develop so radical yet so amazingly clear a picture of the universe?

The real world is hidden from view by veils of negativity, symptoms and appearances. Like kabbalists before him and after, the Ari, Isaac Luria, the "Lion of Safed," along with his fellow kabbalists, found the answer, at least in part, in the blueprint provided for us by the cosmic code known as the Bible.

When you come to the land of Canaan... and I put a plague of leprosy in a house of the land of your possessions, etc.[15]

The Canaanites were of a negative, evil consciousness, and whenever they erected a building they made use of and connected with evil forces that roam at random throughout the universe, and made these evil forces become expressed within the building. When a person begins to set up a building he should declare that he is building it for the service of the Force.

The Lord loved the Israelites and brought them into the Holy Land to place his divine Force among them and to make His abode with them, so that Israel should be wholly above all else.

> Now, when the women brought articles for the Tabernacle they used to "specify what part each was for... and all the women whose heart stirred them up in wisdom..."[16] The women with wisdom understood the power of the mind and human activity. They were stirred up in wisdom and each thing connected with the Force.[17]

What seems to emerge from the Biblical narration is the direct relationship that exists between the inanimate reality and its constant interaction on the most subtle levels. The kabbalist knows that all events on the physical level are directed by an internal energy force of intelligence which evolves into that which we observe in manifest form.

Herein lies the essential difference between the world view of the Kabbalist and the scientist. Everything and everyone has a level and frame of intelligence and consciousness, including the rock or a table. A table talks, and so does food. One seated in a restaurant where the previous occupant of the table threw off enormous negative vibrations becomes very uncomfortable during the meal and never knows why. A house with negative vibrations[18] talks and may make a new purchaser or tenant agitated. The table and the house have intelligence.

Whether we are conscious of their intrinsic language or we do not understand the language of the inanimate inhabitants of our universe, they reveal much of what is going on around us. The Kabbalist or student of Kabbalah knows perfectly well that a home, apartment or business that became corrupted by negative, evil conscious human beings, is a place to stay away from. The Kabbalist will pick up the intelligence of these inanimate entities and act appropriately.

Every vessel of an inanimate structure has a certain note that causes it to reverberate louder than at any other frequency. Gently encircle the rim of a wine glass with a moistened finger to find that vessel's resonant harmonic. The trick of breaking wine glasses is accomplished by singing that particular pitch at a volume sufficient to cause the glass to explode from the force of its own vibrations.

As to the matter of trees, and their relationship to *Tu B'Shevat*, the fifteenth day of lunar Aquarius, it should be noted that the desire of the plant kingdom, while in a surprising number of ways similar to that of animal and man, does not reveal as pronounced an individuality of consciousness. A plant cannot, by and within itself, possess the mobility inherent in human and animal realities. Still, plants, unlike rocks, do react physically to the stimuli of sunlight, water, heat and cold.

Many celestial energies function according to strict annual cycles. According to the ruling of Bet Hillel, the New Year for trees is on the fifteenth of lunar Aquarius. It is on this day that trees receive their yearly infusion of celestial energy and a miraculous birth and spectacular potential for new growth becomes revealed.

Rosh Hashana or New Year is not merely an occasion for best wishes for another year. Nor, as many people think, is it merely a tradition in which all humankind is judged on the basis of past year's activity. The fundamental idea behind the Rosh Hashana code is that on that particular day of the year, the four kingdoms or levels of consciousness receive their infusion from the Force. Without this new lease on life, all of the four phases would perish.

The energy consciousness of the tree is one of restriction, as that term is described by Kabbalah. When the restrictive consciousness becomes manifest, the energy-intelligence (be it that of a man or of a tree) resists external limitations as it strives to reach its full potential. The tree, with its inherent restrictive consciousness, repels the efforts of Earth's Desire to Receive. Despite her consciousness of gravitational desire, Earth herself is powerless to restrain or prevent a tree's upward growth.

The benefits of the fifteenth day come about through the mating and unification of Moon (Malkhut) with Sun (Ze'ir Anpin).[19] The fifteenth day incorporates a variety of powerful energy-intelligences which can be tapped by those with a proper attitude of restriction. Such energies can go a long way in promoting the welfare and success of any new venture or undertaking.

The Age of Aquarius, an age of unification and humanity to our fellow man, will contribute to a model of a grand unification of all mankind. No longer will the cosmos and man, the inanimate and the animate, be understood as isolated entities, but rather as integrated elements. Lunar Aquarius embodies a power of circuitry in which all things and events will be revealed as interdependent and inseparable parts of the cosmic whole.

It is not an individual that brings "peace on earth and good will towards our fellow man." When the collective consciousness of all of mankind is brought together, and a pure awareness of the intrinsic wholeness of reality is achieved, then, and only then, will this force, the collective consciousness, prepare itself for the final onslaught on the negative aspect of desire: desire to receive for the self alone. Only then will the Messiah make his appearance and bring about the Messiah consciousness, the grand unification of mankind.

# Why

*do some days have
the power of positive energy
and other days the opposite?*

LET US NOW TURN TO THE COSMIC INFLUENCES THAT CONTROL
our activities and influence our lives on a day to day basis. Is
there one particular day of the week in which our friendly skies
most strongly echo a future of success? Yes, declares the Zohar,
and that day is Tuesday.

Beginning with nightfall on Monday and continuing until
sundown on Tuesday, positive energy-intelligences are prevalent
in our cosmos. Why nightfall? The answer according to the Ari,
Rabbi Isaac Luria, is to be found in the dictum of Returning
Light.[1]

Since the Desire to Receive, which had been established in
the Endless (*En Sof*), was receiving continuously the infinite
beneficence of the Force, there arose among the vessels (the
undifferentiated souls of humanity) a feeling known to Kabbalah
as Bread of Shame. The problem was, the vessels were

receiving endlessly of the Force's abundance but could do nothing to repay the Force's kindness, inasmuch as the Force, being whole and lacking nothing, has no Desire to Receive. Thus the vessels experienced Bread of Shame[2] at being unable to earn the blessings it was receiving.

To alleviate this situation, the Force withdrew its blessing from the vessels, creating a situation such that where there was Light the vessels would see only darkness, and since that day only by restricting the Desire to Receive could the vessel remove Bread of Shame and again return to the Light.

Thus was established the paradox of opposites and the concept of Returning Light.[3] Such is the nature of this paradox, that in order to effect a flow of energy and fulfill the Desire to Receive, the vessel must reject that which it most desires. The removal of Bread of Shame requires rejection. The vessel, in other words, which desires nothing more than to receive the Light's blessing, must reject the Light.

When faced with opposites we usually focus on their differences and not on their affinities. The idea of an intrinsic unity of opposites is foreign to our way of thinking. But from a kabbalistic perspective, the two poles of a magnet are merely different aspects of the same unified, all-embracing Force. Indeed, it is only when you pull two magnets apart that the difference between them becomes evident.

In truth, the creation of *Ze'ir Anpin*, the force of light in our solar system, preceded the moon, or *Malkhut*, the reflector. However, even sunlight must remain unrevealed until there is a receiving vessel to reflect or restrict it. The only light we ever see is reflected. Deep space is totally dark. Why? Because there is nothing there with which the light from the stars can interact. The light is there, we just can't see it. For a light bulb to glow, the filament must reject the current that is invited by the negative pole in order to reveal light.

From here, it is but a small conceptual step to the idea that the reflector, the vessel, Returning Light, is in a sense the creator of our terrestrial universe and all that it contains. Returning Light permitted the Force to become established. Without Returning Light the Force remains unrevealed. Thus, in essence, Returning Light, at least from the perspective of our illusionary physical realm, appears as the first, causative activity, while the Force appears to be the second, the effect.

To be connected with the Force, one must learn the art and concept of Returning Light. This essential law, which functions both on the physical and metaphysical levels, emerged from the process of creation and will remain in place until our cycle of correction is complete.

Thus we see why Genesis I indicates the day begins with nightfall and concludes at sundown the next day.

And there was evening and there was morning, one day.[4]

Each day complies with the exact formula of cosmic intervention, the day follows the night, the sun follows the moon. The cosmic code of Genesis provides us with a dictum firmly established in the process of creation. However, the cosmic code of the Bible, which provides a detailed description of the entire celestial network, must be decoded (i.e. revealed through resistance), a chore left to the kabbalist.

The physical universe functions in reverse order. While in the true reality level cause precedes effect, positive precedes negative, Sun precedes Moon, in our illusionary physical level of consciousness, effect precedes cause, negative precedes positive, and the Moon begins the day followed by the Sun. So declares the Cosmic Code, without which the Bible and our universe would forever have remained unrevealed.

Vision is but one of many ways that we perceive the world, but our eyes function by the principle of "mirror vision." Everything around us is viewed by our eyes in opposition to that which is ultimately seen, similar to the manner in which the word "AMBULANCE" is painted in reverse on the front of the vehicle named. A driver looking through the rear view mirror, reads the word "AMBULANCE" correctly, from left to right, although it is printed from right to left. A similar situation exists with regard to our perceptions of the world.

The Moon, according to the Zohar, represents the female mode of consciousness, the Sun is male. The Moon has no light of her own, only what she receives from the Sun. At the same time, each day's cosmic activity begins with the appearance of evening, or Moon. A parallel can be drawn in the union of a man and a woman. The first act in the process of the creation of a child is the release of sperm by the man. However the revelation of the union, the child, is accomplished by the mother.

Esoteric and mystical traditions surrounding day three of creation abound with interpretations and tales. The idea of Tuesday, which is synonymous with the biblical third day of creation, representing the grace of the Lord, has long been a part of Jewish heritage. There are many who will move into a new home or begin a new venture on Tuesday. The reason this tradition still maintains a mystical hold on its believers is often attributed to the repetition of the declaration, "And the Lord saw that it was Good."[5]

This affirmation of the Lord's blessings was stated once on the first day, twice on the third day, once on the fourth day, once on the fifth day, and twice on the sixth. No such assertion was made on Day Two. The question that must be raised is why did the Lord declare Tuesday as a good day, and state this assertion, not once but twice?

The third day was forged from two dimensions, the right column and left column. The Lord, on the third day, addressed the right column as now being "good." The third day (Tuesday) was also infused with the cosmic power of restriction, which is the dimension of the central column. The central column energy-intelligence creates a unification between the right and left columns[6] whose internal energy-intelligences are constantly at odds. But on Tuesday the energy-intelligences of both the right and left, positive and negative, were manifested with purposeful light and brilliance.[7]

With a Zoharic perspective of Biblical creation, the whole of Genesis takes on new meaning. Each day of creation reveals a new dimension, or framework of energy intelligence.

In the Western world, our first exposure to the question of why and how life originated often comes through the biblical account of Genesis. However, the Genesis version of the creation of the universe in seven days is vague concerning what exactly happened. The Zohar asserts repeatedly that the Bible is a cosmic code. From seemingly insignificant biblical tales the zoharic and hence the kabbalistic interpretation of creation emerges.

According to the cosmic code, Tuesday emerges as the most powerfully balanced day of the week. The perfect day for a wedding or moving into a new home or apartment. No other day can provide the initial step with a greater focus than Tuesday, which is synonymous with the third day of creation. Should Lag B'omer, the fifteenth day of Av, or the fifteenth day of any Lunar month, fall on a Tuesday this further increases the celestial positive energy-intelligence of the day. However, I must caution the reader that the cosmic influence of a certain day, be it Tuesday or any other, is not sufficient to override more powerful negative cosmic influences.

Do not be persuaded by the surgeon to perform the surgery on a day connected with our danger zones. In all the years that I have been associated with the Centre, among thousands of cases, I have never once seen an occasion in which a physician could not change the date, or the attorney involved in a new venture make himself available for another day.

When we have become convinced of the effectiveness of celestial influences, when we are one with the cosmos and its activity, it becomes quite apparent and truly amazing as to how our mind consciousness begins to affect our environment, and this includes our physician and our lawyer.

It already has been noted that we should avoid Monday and Wednesday unless a more powerful cosmic event takes place on these two days. With respect to Sunday, Thursday, and Friday, the assertion "and it was good" indicates that if for whatever reason, Tuesday is not available for the start of a new venture, then these three days can be considered appropriate positive cosmic frameworks.

The negative energy-intelligence expresses itself as a desire to receive, the positive as a desire to share. The two are brought together through the medium of central column transformation, that of restriction. Sharing requires restraint. Even the doctrine of sharing or charity has its limitations. In his code of Law, Rabbi Joseph Karo makes the point that while ten percent of earnings should be earmarked for charity, one cannot contribute without limit. That limit, declares Karo, is twenty-percent. Any contribution beyond that limit is an "abuse" of energy-intelligence.[8]

Biblical Day One, synonymous with Sunday, describes a universe where all manifestations, physical and metaphysical, are tied together in a web of interconnected relationships, each apart from, yet part of the all-embracing unity. Day One combines all of the seven energy intelligent forces into one unified whole, the seven days being coded expressions of the seven lower sfirot or energy forces. Day One describes the universe as it was in a unified state, before the advent of space-time. Hence the reason for the single assertion of "it was good."

Before the beginning there existed only one unified expression, such as a seed embodies the root, trunk, branches, and leaves of a tree. This is the nature of Day One. It has been argued, therefore, that as Day One contains within itself all future energies, including Day Three, Sunday and not Tuesday is the most appropriate day for beginning new ventures.

Concerning this, the Zohar declares that, "The third day of creation is the code name for the sfirotic energy-intelligence, Tifereth. The Sfira Tifereth encapsulates the dominion of the third column over the other two energy-intelligences.[9] The earth and its entire physical framework came into existence on the third day of existence, which is symbolized by the Sfira Tifereth."[10]

The physical universe came into being when the third force, the mediating principle of restriction known in Kabbalah as the third column, came into existence. Consequently, the biblical code asserts the dynamic physical disclosure of earth's creation with a dual "that it was good" expression, indicating, Tuesday, the embodiment of the awesome power of circuitry, the Force. The third day was good indeed. Therefore, day one follows days three and six in importance as channels for the awesome power of the cosmos.

A clue to an interpretation of the days of the week and its cosmic influence is provided by the Zohar.

And the Lord saw all that he had made, and behold it was very good.[11] Here the word "very" establishes a good reason as to why the words "that it was good" were omitted in the account of the second day. On the second day, *death* was created. But according to our colleagues, the expression "very good" on the sixth day refers also to death.[12]

And behold it was very good, included the Angel of Death. How could it be that the sixth day (Friday), the day the Angel of Death was created, should be considered good? Herein is the mystery of mysteries. The Angel of Death is indeed good: "Because, since all men know that one day they must die, many turn to repentance from fear of him before the Lord."[13]

Because man and woman were created on the sixth day[14] the Angel of Death serves a worthwhile purpose. On the second day, when Death was created, male and female were not as yet present.[15] Death, on this second day, portrayed one aspect, a cosmic internal energy-intelligence of negativity. Yet, the sixth day contains an assertion "And the Lord saw that it was good." Why? The Zohar states: "When the Lord created the world, all was prepared for the coming of Man, who is the king of this world. Man was fashioned to walk in the straight path, as it is written:[16] "The Lord hath made man upright but they have sought out many inventions."[17]

The sixth day was crowned with the Lord's ultimate purpose of Creation, mankind. A day of purpose and the crowning glory of the Force which infused this day with a positive energy-intelligent influence of "good." Another reason, for day six receiving the attribute "good" lies in its position within the Star of David.[18] Each day was imbued with a particular energy force. The sixth day was the Sfira of Yesod (Foundation). As such, she exercised the same cosmic influence as day three, with one exception. Day three's coded position was contained in the upper triad, known as the Tree of Life or metaphysical realm of cosmic consciousness. Day six already related to the lower triad of consciousness located in the Tree of Knowledge dimension.

While day three and day six were both infused with central column energy-intelligence, day three, nonetheless, contained a more purified form of consciousness. Situated within the upper triad of Magen David, she expressed and made manifest a greater degree of pure awareness and cosmic positive expression.

The two days left for consideration are Sunday and Thursday. If no other choice is available which day does the Zohar consider preferable? Before we come to the essential ingredient of the force of these two days, let us consider this Zohar:

> The word Bereshit[19] points towards an esoteric explanation, *Bara Shith*, he created six. From the end of heaven to the end thereof. These six Sfirot (energy-intelligences) are *Hesed, Gevurah, Tifereth, Netzah, Hod* and *Yesod*; *Malkhut*, Earth, is the seventh sfira.[20]

Each day, then, represents a particular, unique energy-intelligence. Day One symbolizes the power of sfira, Hesed.[21] The two fundamental and seemingly opposing forces, which manifest in innumerable ways, including the seeming attraction and repulsion of the poles of a magnet, are not really distinct forces but in *Hesed* are unified and become manifest as one embracing whole.

> The Lord saw the Light that it was good.[22] This is the central column. *Ki Tov* (that it was good) balanced above and below and on all other sides. The power of restriction restores the two opposite forces into a cosmic whole.[23]

What seems to emerge from the Zohar is that the energy-intelligence[24] of central column became manifest on the first day, establishing a balance between positive and negative. Therefore, Sunday is cosmically a balanced, "good day." Unlike Tuesday, however, the two opposing forces were not individually infused with the energy-intelligence of the central column. They were merely placed in a position of a unified cosmic whole and therefore referred to with one assertion, "that it was good." On day one, the two opposing forces were placed in a state of potential balance, not as yet manifested. They were part of and dominated by, the central column energy-intelligence.

Although the metaphysical world seems detached from the physical world, there is no logical requirement for them to remain separated. All aspects of physical existence are merely the messengers of the reality realm of the potential, metaphysical frames of expression. In this critical Age of Aquarius, it benefits us greatly to become fully aware of the dynamics of cosmic influences. For when we have become convinced of the effectiveness of celestial influences, when we are one with the cosmos and its activity, it becomes apparent how truly amazing is our ability to affect our environment through our consciousness.

*Why*

*is day five (Thursday)
considered the opportunity
for self-healing?*

THE KABBALIST SEEKS TO SEPARATE THE WRONG FROM THE
right, the fraudulent from the true — not an easy task in this
era of symptoms, false fronts and second guesses. One of the
main purposes for studying Kabbalah is to remove ourselves
from limited frames of reference. Following upon the heels of
an old kabbalistic doctrine that the light precedes the darkness,
the Zohar presents us with a startling proposal, namely that the
healing process precedes the illness.

Here again we find the kabbalistic revelation that our
universe functions in reverse logic. That we are not the initiators
of our actions, but rather channels for action that is in need of
revealment, runs counter to everything we have ever been led to
believe. Yet, this strange concept, which carries over to the idea
that the cure exists prior to the malady, is woven through the
very fabric of kabbalistic teaching. It is no coincidence that

alongside poison ivy is often found growing its antidote Jewelweed.

To come to a better understanding of this concept and how it relates to the topic at hand, let us explore the coded declaration concerning the fifth day, "it was good." An apt starting point for our investigation is the coded information provided by the word *Tov*, meaning good. For this we must again appeal to the profound aspect of the Hebrew alphabet which describes how energy-intelligences are made manifest, how they pervade space, and their crucial role in the four kingdoms.[1]

The word Tov (good) is a code name for the Force when it becomes manifest at all three levels or columns of expression, left, right, and central. The letters, Tet, Vav and Beth in the word Tov encompass the Force at *all* its levels. The *upper world*, known by its code name *Yisrael Savah V'Tvunah*, is portrayed by the letter Tet. The letter Vav represents the coded consciousness of *Ze'ir Anpin*. The letter Beth embodies the upper and lower phases of *Malkhut*, the World of Action.[2] Together, these three letters are expressions of the *sfira* of *Yesod*, Foundation.[3]

The fifth day is the coded energy-intelligence of sfirotic Hod consciousness, which embodies the left column aspect of the all-embracing unified whole. The zoharic interpretation of Tov (good) reveals that the mediating attribute, the middle column is apparently not functional within Hod consciousness. Certainly, the first, third and sixth days, in which the energy-intelligence of the three unified columns became expressed, deserve the assertion of Tov. But why is the fifth day also credited with the attribute of "it was good"?

The Zoharic interpretation of Genesis I presents us with the revelation that day five gave birth to the energy-intelligence of healing. This was due to the advanced knowledge that man, created on day six, would commit offenses against the Force. At the time of creation, the Force would be obliged to withdraw from man and thereby cause a lack of positive energy flow. However, as the Force is omnipresent, a cure would be forever present within the cosmos, even in advance of man's negative activity, and it would remain in place, regardless of man's awareness of it, or lack thereof.[4]

The energy-intelligence of the left column consistently desires to cancel out that of the right column. The right column preceded the left column in the creative process.[5] Its energy-intelligence thus desires to cancel the strength of negative energy-intelligence and permanently subdue it, according to the same principle which governs the seed, the root and the branch.[6]

A Zoharic examination of the master plan of creation reveals many discrepancies, one of which is the creation of the birds and the beasts on day five and its repetition in the second biblical account in chapter two.[7] The reason for this is simply that first biblical account of creation represents creation when it was still in a potential state, the second refers to the physical world.

In Genesis I we read, "Let the waters teem with moving creatures, that have life, and let birds fly above the earth in the open firmament of heaven."[8]

The kabbalist prophet, Rabbi Shimon, tells us that this is a mystical allusion. "Birds" refers to the angel Michael. "To fly" refers to the angel Gabriel, of whom it is written, "The man Gabriel whom I had seen at first in a vision being caused to fly quickly."[9] Of the phrase, "Above the earth," Rabbi Abba says: "this is Raphael (healer of the Force) who is charged to heal the earth so as to furnish an abode for man who he heals of his maladies."[10]

Further elaboration on this subject is found in the zoharic mystical order of curing.

"From the east direction comes another light that contains all forms and aspects of healing which embody the Force and always presents itself to fulfill the wishes of the Force in advance of the illness which later becomes manifest. The desire of the Force is in a constant state of sharing and healing. The name of this light is Raphael"[11]

The Force, though voluntarily sidelined by the Bread of Shame dictum, is restored by the Raphael energy-intelligence that attaches itself to the Force. Raphael consciousness embraces the Force and acts as a channelling mechanism, while at the same time concealing its internal energy-intelligence, the Force. The purpose of Raphael consciousness is to restore the Force to its proper exalted position within the cosmos. The idea behind this cosmic procedure is referred to as the *Tikune* (correction) process. The Darkness recognizes the Light as its sustenance. As such, the forces of darkness lay in wait for the moment when humankind commits offenses against each other and immediately seizes the opportunity to draw power for its nourishment.

Raphael consciousness is continually ready to confront the forces of darkness, which include both universal and individual maladies, but it must await its activation by the restriction of man. We and we alone control the starting switch of Raphael's spacecraft. The activating mechanism remains under the control of the human mystery of restrictive power.

As with everything in the coded text of the Bible, the central message is packaged with others. Witness Adam's first assigned task in the Garden of Eden:[12] "And out of the ground the Lord formed every beast of the field, and every fowl of the air: and brought them unto Adam to see what he would call them: and whatsoever Adam called every living creature that was the name thereof."

The exercise was designed to do far more than keep Adam occupied and insulate him from ennui. Of all the fears that bedevil mankind, none is so terrifying as fear of the unknown. Because what is unknown can neither be avoided nor controlled. By naming the creatures of a newly formed world, Adam became the master of his environment. He was not the last of his line to wield the power of a name.[13] According to the Zohar, Adam was the first and only human at the time of creation with the ability to control the vast universe.

When a man chooses not to restrict he remains in a world of darkness and illusion. The Force that never ceases to flow becomes transferred to negative cosmic zones and consequently pollutes the immediate environment of the transgressor. Man's wrongdoing leads the cosmos to a state of galactic imbalance.

The Lord, or the Force, has but one desire, and that is to infuse the cosmos, including man, with as much positive energy as is necessary to maintain balance and stability. However, because of Bread of Shame, the Force, of necessity, made the appearance of withdrawing. The Light, in its infinite wisdom, concealed Itself to allow us the opportunity of restriction and the removal of Bread of Shame.[14]

The Force never rests. It is forever compelling us toward the culmination of the cosmic process, the re-revealment of the Force, the Tikune. When man sins, succumbing to the Desire to Receive for Oneself Alone, the Desire to Receive nevertheless has drawn the energy of the Force. When humankind desires, the Force always fulfills. However, if man's desire does not include the filament, the obligation to restrict in order to alleviate Bread of Shame, the Light is not revealed, and the void is filled with Klippot, evil energy-intelligences. Thus human activity has the potential to provide nourishment to the cosmos or disruption.

The negative pole of a light bulb is united with its positive counterpart by the filament. The filament provides the necessary restrictive energy-intelligence for a circuit flow of energy. When and if the filament fails to function, a short circuit is the result.[15]

Similarly, man must maintain an activity of restriction, a central column consciousness to retain a circuit flow of energy. Otherwise, the flow of energy comes to a halt and man becomes drained.

But where, at the time of filament failure, has the electric current drawn by the bulb gone? The negative pole has drawn current. Where is it? It has been transferred to the negative cosmic zones portrayed by the black spots that appear at the time of filament failure. Unlike man, whose activity affects the entire universe, the bulb and all entities included within the other three kingdoms[16] do not influence nor cause a quantum effect.

The Commandments and biblical injunctions are seen by the kabbalist as something more than merely the framework of religion or tradition. They are considered for their cosmic significance and importance. The Bible is about the impact of the penetrating Force of the Lord as it makes its way towards physical expression.

Take the biblical prohibition, "Thou shalt not steal." Here, the kabbalistic principle that desire is the root of all corruption is clear. Yet desire, in and of itself, is not a sinful malediction. It is also the source of all correction. Few would condemn a man who steals a loaf of bread, if it was needed to stave off starvation. The desire to feed one's family certainly is not evil, even if one has thought of stealing to do so. One is not to be judged for evil thoughts. Who are we, who have never known this circumstance, to judge? This idea is expressed beautifully by Hillel, the Sage of the Talmud.[17]

What, then is the real meaning of this precept? A good starting point for our investigation is the Hebrew word designating this cosmic process, which is *Averot*. The root meaning of this designation for sin is "transfer." How do we reconcile the word "transfer" to the doctrine of Sin?

When a man succumbs to the negative aspect of desire and steals to serve some greedy end, he blackens and pollutes his cosmic zones. The Force is thus transferred and short-circuitry results. If however the man is motivated by the positive aspect of desire there is no transference and the Force stays with him. Consequently, sin is not a transgression, but rather a transfer of the Force, and punishment is not something meted out by the Lord, but rather by one's failure to restriction.

Of course, one should not steal. Crime, in the long run, really does not pay. But the reason for not stealing should not be merely fear of punishment or imprisonment. The reason for not stealing is simply that the long term liabilities vastly outweigh the short term illusionary gains.

Religion, as it is conventionally misunderstood, does little to alleviate the problems of daily life. In fact, if anything, it is an obstacle on the path to spirituality. With this in mind, it only stands to reason that religion would be widely perceived as a useless impediment towards the enrichment of one's goals and ideals.

Laws and moral and ethical injunctions are ways by which we seek to remedy the situation of greed, but laws, no matter how strictly enforced, do not prevent crime. Nor are moral and ethical injunctions, no matter how noble their intentions, effective at curbing the greedy appetites of man. Taken literally, even the efficacy of the Ten Commandments must be questioned with respect to their attributable results, if any, on the actions of the human race. Man still lies, cheats, steals and kills. In the three millennia that the Ten Commandments have been with us, greed, murder, and covetousness has not abated one iota. If anything it has increased. There seems to be no limit to man's inhumanity to man. A few are blessed with clear conscience — a blessed few.

Why are some of us serving life sentences in a kind of self-imposed purgatory, while others seem to roam free? The simple answer is that some people live within a circular context. This means that they have managed to transform the Desire to Receive for themselves into a Desire to Receive for the Sake of Imparting, while others have not.

We are born with a metaphysical blueprint established in previous lives. This blueprint or karmic X-ray, includes illnesses as well as the power of healing those illnesses. That power is restriction. When radiologists report positive readings in their X-rays, what they note is the black, dark or hazy spots. These spots represent the Force transferred to a danger zone within the body. All internal medical impairments are the direct result of body short-circuitry. By the application of the human filament, restriction, the healing force of the Raphael energy-intelligence splices that part of our metaphysical X-ray which incorporates all forms of darkness. This may include an accident, illness or other negativity stored in our cosmic danger zones.

Most of us live in a robotic-consciousness which prevents us from making contact with tomorrow. The only room for free will, our only opportunity to participate in our future is the extent of our ability to restrict the negative aspect of desire. With restriction, we activate the cosmic splicing mechanism that can alter our future and provide a security shield that removes the already determined cassette initiated by our prior incarnation. The future is here today.

While the Force, governed by the doctrine of Bread of Shame, must not invade our space, nevertheless, the brief contact made with our Desires to Receive, and our inability to activate our human filament reality creates short-circuitry. This dark moment of a prior lifetime must undergo the Tikune process in a future lifetime.[18] The question whether we are masters of our destiny and thus "consciously" activate our filament or fall under the iron fist of "robotic consciousness" is determined by prior life activities.

Unfortunately, for too long, the penetration of this mysterious realm of healing had been left to the few initiated kabbalists. In our Age of Aquarius, the power of the Aleph Beth has become the domain of the people. As such, Day Five now takes on a greater significance. Mankind can now look forward to a future of self-healing. The Bible provides the code. Together with the Zohar, the Kabbalah provides the means of deciphering.

While other days provide a continuous outpouring of cosmic influence, Day Five must await the initiative of mankind. Only through man's restriction does a unity between the Force and Raphael consciousness become a reality. Thus it takes its position as the least of the favorable days of the week in which to initiate a new venture or undertaking.

Day Five is unique among the days of the "friendly skies" in that she does not provide a spontaneous channelling of the awesome power of the Force.[19] Rather, she combines and embodies only the potential power of the Force.

The rest is up to us.

# *What*

*is the nature
of the condition of
immortality?*

THE MOST IMPORTANT CHARACTERISTIC OF THE KABBALISTIC view of the cosmos — one could almost say the essence of it — is the awareness of the mutual interrelatedness between cosmic influence and individual well-being. From the kabbalist's perspective, all things and events are seen as different expressions of the same ultimate reality.

It is to Moses that Kabbalah traces its roots and to whom it owes its existence. The first truths gleaned by the kabbalist had to do with the forces in the universe that can assist as well as annihilate mankind.

> And Moses saw an Egyptian smiting a Hebrew... And he looked here and there.[1]

Moses looked into the fifty letters (*Kriat Shema*) by which the Israelites proclaim the all-embracing cosmic unity. He perceived through elevated consciousness that no good son would ever be born from the Egyptian and so Moses killed him. Moses brought about the death of the Egyptian through the power of the cosmic force "by merely staring at him."[2]

Moses gave the mystical energy of the Bible to the world. Despite many setbacks he never faltered, always he persevered. It was Moses who transformed a horde of slaves into a nation with the potential ability of securing peace and harmony in the world.[3] The Bible attests to his unique power, when the Lord declares, "Hear now my words: My servant Moses is trusted in all my house. With him I speak mouth to mouth and not dark speeches."[4]

The Zoharic view of our universe transcends and occupies a frame beyond space-time. The kabbalistic vision of reality is based on an in-depth perception of the Bible's coded narrations and tales. It emphasizes the energy-intelligent system referred to in the Bible as the Tree of Life.[5]

Did Moses die? The Bible says: "and the Lord buried him in the Land of Moab, but no man knoweth of his sepulchre unto this day."[6] The Zohar, however, states, incredible as it may seem, that Moses did not die. His cosmic bond with the Tree of Life reality was never severed, as was the case with the Israelites after the Golden Calf.[7] Had the Israelites not sinned, their cosmic connection with the Tree of Life would have eternally remained, and their days on earth would have been prolonged forever.

Rabbi Elazar said: "The Lord will one day reestablish the world and strengthen the spirit of the sons of men so that they may prolong their days forever. As it is written:[8] 'For as the days of a tree so shall be the days of my people, ....'"

According to the Zohar, Moses was "gathered in" from this world and caused the Moon to shine, in the form of Joshua, who represented the Moon. For Moses was as the Sun, which also after it sets continues to give light to the Moon. The body of Moses was transported to Heaven and was not seen after his death. Moses, together with Elijah the prophet were again seen alive when they appeared before Rabbi Shimon Bar Yohai and his son Rabbi Elazar in the cave of P'quin where the revelation of the Zohar took place.[9]

It is said that Rabbi Shimon was visited twice a day by the prophet Elijah. The deeper and more comprehensive sections, known as the *Ra'ya Mehemna*, are a record of the discourses that took place between Rabbi Shimon and Moses himself, the faithful shepherd. According to the ancients, these meetings took place hundreds of years after their departure from the Earth. It is said that a cloud or chariot was continually with them for their return to Earth or their journey to outer space. They did not die, but would remain as the Sun, which after setting does not expire, but rather continues to give light to the Moon. Righteous individuals, according to the Bible and the Zohar, have always been instrumental in helping humankind.[10] The awesome power of Moses will be with us forever and available for mankind's benefit.

What is the significance of the zoharic comparison of Moses to the Sun?

Like the Sun, which in setting no longer appears in the heavens, the energy-intelligence that is Moses, too, creates this kind of illusion. As the Sun continues to display its eternal beneficence somewhere, so does the energy that once manifested as Moses make its presence felt without interruption. Like the Sun, where the illusion of its setting may be countered by a jet plane, following its path around the world, so can we maintain a continuous spiritual connection with Moses through an uninterrupted demonstration of restriction consciousness.

We find this awareness of Moses and his channelling of the Force demonstrated in many areas of kabbalistic teachings, the most famous of which is related to the Holiday of Purim and also to the evil Haman, chief minister of the Persian King, Ahasuerus.

And it was known that Haman, the wicked, was a great astrologer, as indicated in the verse: "In the first month, which is the month of Nissan (Aries) in the twelfth year of King Ahasuerus, Haman cast an astrological chart from day to day, and from month to month, to the twelfth month, which is the month of Adar."[11]

When he determined that the chart of Moses fell on the month of Adar (Pisces), Haman rejoiced greatly, exclaiming: "The chart has fallen for me on the month in which Moses died!" He did not know, however, that although Moses died on the seventh day of Adar, he was also born on that day.[12]

For Haman, the astrological star chart was a signpost in achieving his evil objective.[13] Thus, on the seventh day of lunar Adar (Pisces), this day reflected an evil sign for Israel, the day that Moses died. However, what Haman and conventional astrology as well failed to notice, was that while so righteous a person as Moses left this physical, illusionary reality on the seventh day of lunar Pisces, he also came into this universe on the same day.

"And the people came out of the Jordan on the tenth day of the first month (lunar Aries)."[14] On the seventh day of lunar Aries, three days prior to their crossing the river Jordan, they were told to prepare provisions for their journey. "Then Joshua commanded the officers of the people, saying: prepare provisions for within three days you shall cross the Jordan."[15] For thirty days, the Israelites mourned the death of Moses, as it is written: "And the children of Israel wept for Moses in the plains of Moab thirty days."[16] Subtracting thirty days from lunar Aries traces the death of Moses back to the seventh day of lunar Pisces.[17]

This calculation was also known to Haman, who therefore read into the stars the cosmic omen of death for the Israelites. He failed, however, to grasp the implication of another coded verse in the Bible that would translate his astrological conclusions of death to one of birth and rejoicing.

"And Moses went and spoke these words unto all Israel. And he said unto them: 'I am one hundred twenty years old this day.'"[18] This was the essential piece of information which Haman lacked. When the biblical code inserted the word "this day," the Bible was confirming another doctrine that would assist mankind in its pursuit of freedom and well-being.

Did the birth of Moses on this particular day place emphasis of joy within the day? Or did the cosmos, on the seventh day of lunar Pisces, generate an enormous power of energy-intelligence which infused the human consciousness of a baby known as Moses?

Every event, every action, every idea is connected through the human mind with cosmic power and influence. A day that brought about and produced such a righteous person, an individual of the caliber of a Moses, infuses the entire universe on this day with positiveness. Such a day is the seventh of lunar Pisces, a day most beneficial for the commencement of a new undertaking or venture.

Knowledge is the connection. Genesis spells out the relationship between knowing and connection. "Adam knew Eve, his wife, and she conceived and bore Cain."[19] This goes beyond the mere biological coupling by which mammals reproduce their kind. The case of Adam and Eve might be compared with two people who know the same thing about sports, fashion, physics, or the weather. When they know, they somehow seem to have a greater affinity. Both are connected to the same thing. Consequently, when we know of the cosmos, when we understand cosmic consciousness and its internal energy intelligence, only then do we connect with the true knowledge.

This is why Kabbalistic Astrology goes to such great lengths to provide a connection with cosmic energy rather than merely relying on the natal chart. We are primarily concerned with experiential knowledge. When we connect with the internal and external aspects of cosmic energy, we then are in a position to know the universe and the purpose of our being.

# *How*

*will the teachings
of Kabbalah in this Age
become the tool in the
hands of man to draw
down the light*

ONCE THE BACKBONE OF A VIBRANT CIVILIZATION, RELIGION HAS failed dismally to keep pace with the changing times. Sociologists, law enforcement officials and government planners seem powerless to stem the tide of drugs, AIDS, violent crime and moral disintegration. Small wonder many of us harbor feelings of hopelessness which have almost no precedent in history.

Small wonder that so many of us believe that our form of high-tech civilization eventually must collapse if present trends continue.

Sociologists and government planners now express deep concern about our ability to respond properly to the problems in terms of family, traditions and cultural breakdown. Religion, at one time considered the backbone and support of a vibrant, fulfilling society, has dismally failed to keep pace with the changing times or stemming the tide of social and moral disintegration. Institutions which have been supportive of human relationships are crumbling and becoming meaningless to our society as a whole.

A disease is eating away at the very fibre that once kept families together, existing friendships, and some pride in government. To stress one problem over another is merely a cosmic ploy that prevents us from reaching into the heart and core of a distressing and disturbing human civilization. We must be able to respond to the challenges of an Age of Aquarius and recognize the formidable obstacle which stands in our way.

The concept of "Love thy neighbor as thyself."[1] has had little, if any, impact upon the peoples of this planet. And yet this basic doctrine has been the underlying premise for religion's existence, which I must add, applies to Kabbalah as well. Then, why do I assume, that the teachings of Kabbalah will make the necessary change in our human behavior where others have failed? What is so unique about its message that others do not seem to incorporate?

It is written in the Zohar, the *Book of Splendor*,[2] that Kabbalah would have to await the coming of the Age of Aquarius to make its reappearance as a tool to be wielded by the hands of man, an electronic instrument to draw down Light upon the human race, wandering and confused in cosmic darkness.

Today, more than at any other time in history, the Light is pressing in, demanding revealment. In this, the Messianic Era, the pressure exerted by the Force on humanity will be of such intensity that the Zohar was prompted to declare:

"Woe unto him who meets with this period; praiseworthy is the portion of those who encounter and have the spiritual capacity to be cast with that time."

What this means is that those of us who fail to harness the energy of the Force are doomed to suffer the inevitable consequences of uncertainty, despair, and disease; while those of us who have knowledge of the cosmic forces and who exercise a proper attitude of restriction will be blessed with spiritual grace beyond our wildest imaginings.

Many of our disappointments, frustrations and failures, can be traced to bad timing. Dig to the roots of a failed marriage or business venture and more often than not you will find that the venture began in one of our cosmic danger zones. Awareness of these zones can help us alleviate many problems.

To merely preach for the removal of the barriers of intolerance and hatred is futile. To attempt to patch up our problems with rhetoric is only to delay the inevitable. Industry will not save us. Not commerce, technology, nor military might. The key to change, societal and individual, is consciousness.

Enlightenment means the revelation and manifestation of the all-embracing reality of the Force. By connecting with the reality realm of our consciousness, we cut through the illusion of darkness and reveal the Light. Having succeeded in altering our states of consciousness, we diminish the fundamental problem of the "unknown" which has driven society to the brink of disaster.

In our confused, crisis ridden generation are we in some way better suited to achieve purer awareness and states of elevated consciousness? The answer, confirms the Zohar,is an emphatic yes. The Messianic era will usher in a period of unprecedented enlightenment and information. The layman, who for centuries had been shut-off from information reserved for a few knowledgeable physicists and cosmologists, will easily access into the reservoir of quantum consciousness. The doubts and uncertainties that scientists are beset with, will not in any way affect the ordinary individual. We will experience an information revolution organized by the sea of mankind rather than by our higher institutions of learning.

Now let us return to the question previously raised. Just what is it that Kabbalah shares with mankind that places its teachings on a unique pedestal? The kabbalistic world view reflects the innate harmoniousness of our universe. Like the quantum physicist, the kabbalist understands that human consciousness has the unique ability to influence and even radically alter the physical nature of the universe. Indeed, according to kabbalistic thinking, cosmic influences and man's activity are intimately entwined.

For the Kabbalist, man can never succeed unless he becomes consciously connected with the reality. For the most part, all of mankind have their ties with the world of uncertainty. The argument against certainty or predictability in nature is a basic tenet of Quantum Theory. Heisenberg's Uncertainty Principle established an inherent, inextricable indeterminism in the web of all existence wherever it may occur.

At the root of this dilemma, from the Kabbalistic perspective, lies human free will, the ability or inability to become captain of his ship and master of his destiny. Towards this objective strives the teachings of Kabbalah.

Rather than place the problems of society within a symptomatic frame of reference, the Kabbalah cuts through to the basic problem, which spells out in terms of "why". Why has mankind turned to drugs — medicinal or abusive — in the first place? Why is the individual more vulnerable today to outside influences than ever before. Why do most people complain of stress in their lives despite the many remedies available?

The Zohar states that in the Days of Messiah, there will no longer be the necessity for one to request of his neighbor, "Teach me wisdom" as it is written:[3] "One day they will no longer teach every man his neighbor, and every man his brother, saying know the Force (Lord), for they shall all know Me, from the youngest to the oldest of them."[4]

So in the end we find that the mysterious message of Kabbalah is no mystery at all. With our sights set on the "high road" of reality, we can overcome all obstacles. It is simply a matter of disengaging from the darkness of illusion and becoming consciously connected with reality of the Light.

# Appendices

# References

**Introduction**
1. Zohar II p. 265a.
2. Genesis 1:27.
3. Zohar II, p. 76a.
4. Power of Aleph Beth, vol. I, Berg, pp. 67-81.

**Chapter 1**
1. Genesis, 4:1.
2. Kabbalah for the Layman, Berg, pp. 65-67.
3. Zohar III, p. 99b.
4. Kabbalah for the Layman vol.III, Berg, p. 131.

**Chapter 2**
1. Ten Luminous Emanations, vol.II, R. Ashlag, pp. 81-90.
2. Power of Alpeh Beth, Berg, pp. 57,58.

**Chapter 3**
1. Ten Luminous Emanations, vol.II, R. Ashlag, pp. 76-79.
2. Ten Luminous Emanations, vol.II; Beginners 1 - Tapes, Berg,
   Research Centre of Kabbalah.
3. Kabbalah for the Layman, Berg, pp. 78-80, 86-90.
4. Ten Luminous Emanations, vol. I, R. Ashlag, p. 67
5. Kabbalah for the Layman, Berg, p. 24.

**Chapter 4**
1. Gates of Elevated Consciousness, Rabb Isaac Luria, Research Centre of
   Kabbalah, 1985, p. 10.
2. Gate of Elevated Consciousness, Luria, Research Centre of
   Kabbalah, 1985, p. 5.
3. Implications of Meta-physics for Psycho-energetic systems. Jack Sarfatti
4. Genesis, 4:1.
5. Zohar III, p. 58a.
6. Jeremiah, 31:33.
7. Zohar I, p. 134b.

**Chapter 5**
1. Genesis, 5:5.
2. Genesis, 5:27.
3. Astrology: Star Connection, Berg. pp. 120,147

4. Zohar II, p. 7a-8a.
5. Jeremiah, 31:3.

**Chapter 6**
1. Isaiah, 11:6.
2. Gift of the Bible, Ashlag, Research Centre of Kabbalah, p. 121.
3. Deuteronomy, 18:15; 34:10.
4. Numbers, 12:8.
5. Zohar II, p. 70a
6. Exodus, 18:2,3
7. Ibid, 18:5
8. Book of Jonah, chap 1.
9. Exodus, 17:2-3
10. Midrash Rabbah, Exodus.

**Chapter 7**
1. Deuteronomy, 5:24.
2. Ibid, 5:5.
3. Exodus, 4:15, 16.
4. Zohar II, p. 22b.
5. Exodus, 6:2.
6. Ibid., 5:22.
7. Astrology: Star Connection, Berg. pp. 72-75.
8. Deuteronomy, 18:18,20-22.
9. Deuteronomy, 13:2-4.
10. Ibid, 13:4.
11. Kings I, 13:1-32.
12. Jeremiah, 23:14; Isaiah, 28:7.
13. Ezekiel, 14:9-11.
14. Zohar II, p. 95a.
15. Genesis, 47:28.
16. Zohar I, p. 211b.
17. Kabbalah Connection, Berg, pp. 106,142.
18. Deuteronomy, 18:21-22.
19. Rashi, Deuteronomy 18:22.
20. Genesis, 37:6-10.
21. Zohar I, p.183a.
22. Numbers, 12:6.
23. Genesis, 41:13

24. Space-time and Beyond, E.P. Dutton, 1975.
25. Job, 33:15-16.
26. Zohar I, p. 183a.

**Chapter 8**
1. Astrology: Star Connection, Berg, p. 70
2. Ecclesiastes 1:9
3. Genesis, 4
4. Zohar II, p. 7b.
5. Isaiah, 63:5
6. Zachariah, 13:9.
7. Zohar III, p. 23a.
8. Zohar III, p. 58a.
9. Entrance to the Zohar, Ashlag, Berg ed., pp. 22-27.
10. Ecclesiastes, 7:14.
11. Kabbalah for the Layman vol.II, Berg, p. 72.
12. Kabbalah Connection, Berg, pp. 117-118.
13. Zohar I, pp. 44a, 125a.
14. Zohar III, p. 52b.

**Chapter 9**
1. Zohar II, p. 81b.
2. Zohar III, p.125a.
3. Power of Aleph Beth, vol. II Berg, pp. 37-39.
4. Exodus, 19:16
5. Zohar II, p. 80b.
6. Exodus, 20:15.
7. Deuteronomy, 5:4.
8. Zohar II, p.81a.
9. Exodus, 32.
10. Ezequiel, 38:1-23
11. Astrology: Star Connection, Berg, pp.132-133.
12. Power of Aleph Beth vol. II, Berg, p.65.
13. Genesis, 11:1.
14. Ibid. 11:4.
15. Zohar I, p. 25b.
16. Zohar II, p. 191b.
17. Numbers, 11:4-6.
18. Ibid., 11:11.

19. Exodus, 12:38
20. Numbers, 11:9.
21. Ibid 14:22,23.
22. Ibid 14:29,30.
23. Ibid 14:23.
24. Zohar I, p. 23a.
25. Gates of Reincarnation, R. Luria, p. 52.
26. Zachariah, 14:9-11.
27. Sefer Lekutim, Kitvay Ari, 1989, vol. 18, p.264.

**Chapter 10**
1. Genesis, 1:16-19.
2. Isaiah, 29:14
3. Zohar III, p.281b.
4. Kabbalah for the layman, vol. I, Berg, pp.78-80.
5. Talmud Bavli, Tractate Shabbat, p 53b.
6. Leviticus 13:47-53, 14:33-45.
7. Genesis Rabbah, 10:6.
8. Psalms, 81:4.
9. Zohar III, p. 100b.
10. Talmud Bavli, Tractate Nidah, p. 39b.
11. Neils Bohr
12. Astrology: Star Connection, Berg, pp. 69,70.
13. Talmud Bavli, Tractate Shabbat, p. 156a.
14. Ibid. 156a.
15. Talmud Bavli, Tractate Erubin, p 56a.
16. Astrology: Star Connection, Berg, p.69,70.
17. Proverbs, 10:2
18. Zohar I, p.180b.

**Chapter 11**
1. Joshua 10:14.
2. Ibid 10:12.
3. Astrology: Star Connection, Berg, pp. 69, 70.
4. Genesis 45:3-8.
5. Zohar I, p. 201b.
6. Proverbs, 10:2.
7. Zohar III, p. 111a.
8. Power of Aleph Beth, vol. I, Berg, p. 127.

9. Ibid, p.135
10. Gate of Elevated Consciousness, Luria, RCK, 1989 p. 5.
11. Isaiah, 29:14
12. Zohar III, p. 281b.
13. Introduction, Or Ha'Hama, Abraham Azulai (1570-1643).
14. Zohar I, p.117b.
15. Zephania, 3:9.

**Chapter 12**
1. Zohar III, p. 281b
2. Zohar I, p. 180b
3. Zohar I, p. 180b
4. Jeremiah, 31:33

**Chapter 13**
1. Genesis, 12:1
2. Astrology: Star Connection, Berg, P.49-50.
3. Zohar III, p. 281b.
4. Ibid
5. Exodus, 2:2.
6. Zohar II, p. 12a.
7. Jeremiah, 42:4.
8. Talmud Bavli, Tractate Rosh Hashana, p. 18b.
9. Power of the Aleph Beth, Berg, vol.I, pp. 56-57.
10. Talmud Bavli, Tractate Ta'anith, p.6.
11. Numbers, 33:38.
12. Tractate Ta'anith 4:6.
13. Zohar II, p. 12a.
14. Kabbalah Connection, Berg, p.143.
15. Power of the Aleph Beth, Berg, vol. II, pp.60-61.
16. Power of the Aleph Beth, Berg, vol. I, p.133.
17. Kabbalah for the Layman, vol. I, Berg, pp. 87-90.
18. Fruit of Tree of Life, R. Isaac Luria, Research Centre of Kabbalah,
    vol. 17 p.519.

**Chapter 14**
1. Book of Formation, Research Centre of Kabbalah, 1990.
2. II Kings, 25:7
3. Genesis, 35:19

4. Genesis, 7:11.
5. Kabbalah for the Layman, vol. II, Berg, p. 119.
6. Book of Formation, Rabad, p.9.
7. Genesis, 30:4-6.
8. Book of Formation, Rabad, p.9.
9. Zohar III, p.152a.
10. Astrology, Star Connection, Berg, p. xxii.
11. Numbers, 2:3.
12. Numbers, 2:25.
13. Numbers, 10:33.
14. Zohar p. 155a.
15. Astrology: Star Connection, Berg. pp.161-163.
16. Numbers, 10:14.
17. Ibid, 10:18.
18. Exodus, 27:9
19. Numbers, 10-22.
20. Ibid. 10:25.
21. Zohar III, p. 118b.
22. Power of Aleph Beth, vol. I, Berg, pp.113-122, pp. 204-222.
23. Genesis, 49.
24. Ibid., 49:16-19.
25. Numbers, 10:25.
26. Judges, 13.
27. Zohar I, p. 243b.
28. Kabbalah for the Layman, vol. II, Berg, pp. 88-91.
29. Power Aleph Beth, vol.2 Berg, p.99.
30. Kabbalah Connection, Berg, pp. 101-103.
31. Ecclesiastes, 3:1.

**Chapter 15**
1. Zohar I, p. 134b.
2. Avoth, 3:1.
3. Genesis, 1:26.
4. Song of Songs, 2:12.
5. Power of Aleph Beth, vol.I, Berg, p.178.
6. Genesis, 2:5.
7. Zohar I. p. 97a.
8. Astrology: Star Connection, Berg, pp. 90-91.
9. Deuteronomy, 30:19.

10. Kitvay Ari, Sha'ar Ma'amare Rashbi, vol. 7, p, 7.
11. Isaiah, 40:26.
12. Zohar I, p. 1b.
13. Lamentations, 2:13.
14. Deuteronomy, 30:19.
15. Zohar I, p. 1b.

**Chapter 16**
1. Gates of Meditation, Rabbi Isaac Luria. pp. 310-313.
2. Genesis, 17:4-6.

**Chapter 17**
1. Power of Aleph Beth, Berg, vol.I, pp. 27, 77-79.
2. Kabbalah for the Layman, Berg, vol.I, pp. 126, 127.
3. Kabbalah for the Layman, Berg, vol. II, pp. 100, 101.
4. Zohar I, p. 97b.
5. Ecclesiastes, 7:14.
6. Power of Aleph Beth, vol.2, pp. 89,90.
7. Zohar II, p. 179b.
8. Psalms, 22:20.

**Chapter 18**
1. Talmud Bavli, Tractate Ta'anith, p. 26b.
2. Ibid.
3. Kabbalah Connection,Berg, pp.113-115.
4. Zohar III, p. 100b.
5. Astrology: Star Connection, Berg, pp. 139-140.
6. Power of Aleph Beth, vol.I pp. 157-158.
7. Astrology: Star Connection, pp. 53-54.
8. Kabbalah Connection, Berg, pp. 112-116.
9. Astrology: Star Connection, Berg p. 10.
10. Kabbalah for the Layman, vol II, Berg, pp. 28-30.

**Chapter 19**
1. Talmud Bavli, Tractate Berohot, p. 61b.
2. Kings I 6:1.
3. Chronicles, 3:2, Kings I, 6:1.
4. Zohar III p. 283b.
5. Kabbalah for the Layman vol.I, Berg pp.26-30.

6. Gates of Meditation, R. Isaac Luria, vol. 11 Research Centre of Kabbalah ed., p.190.
7. Numbeis, 1:1.
8. Zohar III, p. 117b.

**Chapter 20**
1. Numbers, 25:9.
2. Talmud Bavli, Tractate Jebamoth, p. 62b.
3. Power of Aleph Beth, vol. I, p.65.
4. Leviticus, 19:18.
5. Zohar III, p. 23a.
6. Jeremiah, 31:34.
7. Micha, 5:6.
8. Kabbalah for the Layman, vol III, Berg, p. 141.
9. Zohar I, p. 203b.
10. Kabbalah for the Layman, vol.III, Berg, pp.177-178.
11. Kabbalah Connection, Berg, pp.130-132.
12. An Entrance to the Zohar, R. Yehuda Ashlag, ed. Berg, pp. 110-116.
13. Kabbalah for the Layman, Berg, pp. 72-73.
14. Kitvay Ari, Tree of Life, R. I. Luria, Research Centre of Kabbalah Edition, 1985 Gate 42, Sec. 1.
15. Leviticus, 14:34.
16. Exodus, 35:26.
17. Zohar III, p.50a.
18. Kabbalah for the Layman, vol.III, Berg, pp. 140-142.

**Chapter 21**
1. Power of Aleph Beth, Berg, vol.I, p.68.
2. Kabbalah for the Layman II, Berg, pp. 133-134.
3. Kabbalah for the Layman III, Berg, pp. 142-146.
4. Genesis, 1:5.
5. Genesis 1:10-12.
6. Kabbalah for the Layman, vol. I, Berg, p.97-98.
7. Zohar I, p. 19b.
8. Code of Law, R. Joseph Karo, Yoreh Deah, 249:1.
9. Zohar I, p. 39b.
10. Zohar I, p.15a.
11. Genesis 1:31.
12. Zohar I, p. 47a.

13. Zohar II, p. 149b.
14. Genesis, 1:27.
15. Ibid.
16. Ecclesiastes, 7:29.
17. Zohar II, p. 150a.
18. Kabbalah for the Layman, vol. I, Berg, p. 170.
19. Genesis, 1:1.
20. Zohar I, p. 15b.
21. Kabbalah for the Layman, vol. I, Berg, p. 115.
22. Genesis, 1:4.
23. Zohar I, p. 16b.
24. Power of Aleph Beth, vol. I, Berg, 180-181.

**Chapter 22**
1. Entrance to the Zohar, Ashlag, pp. 54-58.
2. Power of Aleph Beth, Vol II, Berg, 21.
3. Zohar I, p. 30a.
4. Zohar I, p. 12b.
5. Kabbalah for the Layman, vol.I, Berg, pp. 73-75.
6. Kabbalah Connection, Berg, pp. 23-27.
7. Power of Aleph Beth, vol I, Berg, pp. 182-185.
8. Genesis, 1:20.
9. Daniel, 9:21.
10. Zohar I, p.46a.
11. Zohar II, p. 254.
12. Genesis, 2:19.
13. Power of the Aleph Beth, vol.I, Berg, pp. 173-175.
14. Kabbalah for the Layman, vol. I, Berg, pp. 78-80.
15. Kabbalah Connection, Berg, p.53.
16. Entrance to the Tree of Life, Ashlag, pp. 54-58.
17. Talmud Bavli, Pirkai Avot, chap. 2, p.5.
18. Wheels of a Soul, Berg, 17.
19. Power of Aleph Beth, vol.I, Berg, p. 85.

**Chapter 23**
1. Exodus, 2:11-12.
2. Zohar II, p. 126a.
3. Power of Aleph Beth, vol. I, Berg, pp. 56,57.
4. Numbers, 12:6-8.

5. Entrance to the Tree of Life, Ashlag, ed. Berg, pp. 88-101.
6. Deuteronomy, 34:6.
7. Exodus, 32.
8. Isaiah, 65:22.
9. Tikune, Zohar p.1a.
10. Astrology: Star Connection, Berg, pp. 162-165.
11. Esther, 3:7.
12. Talmud Bavli, Tractate Megillah, p. 13b.
13. Kitvay Ari, Gates of Meditation, Luria, p. 329.
14. Joshua, 4:19.
15. Ibid., 3:2.
16. Deuteronomy, 34:8.
17. Talmud Bavli, Tractate Megillah, Rashi, p.13b.
18. Deuteronomy, 31:1-2.
19. Genesis, 4:1.

**Epilogue**
1. Leviticus, 19:18
2. Zohar II, p.7b.
3. Jeremiah, 31:33.
4. Zohar III, p.58a.

# Index